Cockroaches, God, Death, and Mangoes

PRAISE FOR
COCKROACHES, GOD, DEATH, AND MANGOES

"Leavitt tells this harrowing story with profound attention to detail, drawing the reader into the inner life of then 8-year-old Bikonzi, while setting such intimacy within the context of a larger, often overlooked historical happening. This story of forced displacement—a testament to faith, endurance, and the human spirit—is remarkably hard to believe, making its truthfulness only an addition to its vitality."
-**Mary Kaech**, Exec. Dir., Phoenix Refugee Connections

"We are changed by stories. We are especially impacted by stories of children who defy all odds, find resilience and courage in themselves, and live to tell the story so that others might live. Read this book and fall in love with young Bikonzi. Read it to remind yourself that we belong to a global village, and when children suffer in a Congolese war, we all suffer. Read it to bear witness to survivors who teach us that horror demands revelation and redemption. And read it for change. Bikonzi will envision it for you!"
-**Dr. Kit Danley**, President, Neighborhood Ministries

"Leavitt masterfully tells the story of Bikonzi and his family as they are forcibly displaced from their home. Bikonzi's story captures the pain of displacement, the resilience of the human spirit, and the struggle to find a home in foreign land. It is a sobering, moving account that forces us to look at some of the real people behind one of our major world crises."
-**Rob Dalrymple**, PhD, Executive Director of Determinetruth

"I have had the privilege of knowing Bikonzi personally and hearing his story firsthand. What Leavitt has captured in these pages is not just a harrowing tale of survival, but a stunning testimony of God's mercy amid unimaginable darkness. We move through life wrapped in the rhythms of our own routines, often unaware of the suffering, war, and displacement that so many endure daily. This book is a gift—an opportunity to pause, to witness, and to let our hearts be softened toward those whose pain we might otherwise never see. My hope is that as you read, you will be drawn into greater awareness, deeper compassion, and a renewed understanding of God's presence, even in the hardest places."

-**Olivia Mulerwa**, President, Mission ONE

COCKROACHES, GOD, DEATH, AND MANGOES

THE TRUE STORY OF BIKONZI MOISE

CLINT LEAVITT

NEW YORK
LONDON • NASHVILLE • MELBOURNE • VANCOUVER

COCKROACHES, GOD, DEATH, AND MANGOES

THE TRUE STORY OF BIKONZI MOISE

Published in New York, New York, by Morgan James Publishing. Morgan James is a trademark of Morgan James, LLC. www.MorganJamesPublishing.com

Proudly distributed by Publishers Group West®

ISBN 9781636986852 paperback
ISBN 9781636986869 ebook
Library of Congress Control Number: 2025931750

Cover Design by:
Ale Urquide

Interior Design by:
Chris Treccani
www.3dogcreative.net

DEDICATION

To Zoe

CONTENTS

FOREWORD:

The first time I heard Bikonzi's story, it wasn't in a formal setting or during a moment of deep reflection. It was over lunch, woven casually into the conversation as if he were recounting just another chapter of his life. But as he spoke, the room fell silent. Those of us at the table—colleagues who had worked alongside him for years—were left stunned. We had no idea! We sat there, trying to process what we had just heard. The weight of it, the sheer impossibility of survival, and yet—here he was, sitting among us. Whole. Hopeful. Joyful, even. We were in the presence of a miracle, and we knew it.

What makes Bikonzi's story so extraordinary is not just the suffering he endured but the fact that he is not defined by it. He carries no bitterness or resentment. He speaks not with anger but with gratitude. Not with despair but with faith. His resilience is a testament to the human spirit, and his willingness to relive these painful memories so that he can share them with us is an act of profound courage. But his story would remain untold without storytellers. For as long as humanity has existed, history, wisdom, and truth have been passed down through stories. Stories are how we remember, understand, and connect across time, culture, and experience. And it is why storytellers—those who dare to listen, capture, and pass on what must not be forgotten—have such an important calling.

Leavitt has done just that in this book. He has taken Bikonzi's harrowing journey and preserved it with reverence, care, and an unwavering commitment to truth. He invites us not just to witness but to feel—to step into the shoes of an eight-year-old boy caught in the middle of war and experience the loss, the fear, the survival, and ultimately, the redemption that unfolded. This book is a gift. It gives us the rare opportunity to bear witness to a story that might otherwise be lost—a story of war, loss, and survival, yes, but even more, a story of faith, resilience, and hope. It reminds us that we live in a world where such suffering exists, though we are often too wrapped up in our own day-to-day concerns to see it. It challenges us to pause, to recognize our own privilege, and to truly see those who have endured so much. As you read, I encourage you to do what we did that day at lunch: pause. Sit with the weight of it. Let it sink in. Marvel at the miracle of Bikonzi and his family's survival. And then, let it change you— in the quiet spaces of your heart. Let it shape your compassion, your awareness, and your willingness to see and serve those who suffer.

-**Olivia Mulerwa**, Mission ONE

ACKNOWLEDGEMENTS

It seems unfair—particularly in the case of a book like this one, where I have the privilege of telling a story of the life of a dear friend—to have only my name listed as an authorial credit. This text is not possible without the work of hundreds of diligent, creative, inspiring artists, editors, administrators, and so many more, and a short section of acknowledgements only catches the surface of my indebtedness to each of them.

I'd like to first and foremost begin by thanking Bikonzi: you'll get to read some more about our relationship in the afterword, but speaking directly to him here: thank you is not enough to summarize my gratitude. For your trust in me to help bring this story to life through the written work, your willingness to dive into such formative yet often painful memories, for your honesty and vulnerability, for your years long friendship—thank you. Your story has softened my heart, catalyzed my advocacy, and strengthened my own resolve; I owe so much of who I am today to you. By extension, to the entire Moise family: not only for your inspiring endurance, faith, courage, and openness, but also for your candidness and willingness to share of your distinct parts in this story. I am honored to know each one of you and call you friends and inspiring examples.

Keeping with the personal acknowledgements, thank you to my wife Emily, who for years has allowed me the time and space to write, the encouragement to spur me on, and the truthfulness to tell me when something worked or perhaps didn't work well. You help me to become the writer, thinker, and truth-teller that I am, and I love you. To the rest of my friends and family, who would be too numerous to name here, but who all in one way or another have kept checking in on progress, affirming the value of my writing on the hard days when it seemed like I might have to throw it all away, and who continue to champion this text even now—thank you. Special thanks to my English teachers and professors from high school through undergraduate and graduate studies: Bill Kimsey, Kevin Storey, Jim Helfers, Brian Raftery, and Diane Goodman, Grayson Carter, amongst others—each of you has helped nurture my voice and shaped me into the writer and thinker I am now and am becoming. This doesn't exist without you.

I'd like to extend gratitude to all those who helped in the editing process along the way: a writer is only ever as good as their editor, and if we could illustrate this through metrics, I am confident this book is approximately 78% better because of the team at Kevin Anderson and Associates. Kathleen McIntosh, your insights into this manuscript help managed to transform and streamline the end result while capturing and elevating the central themes, ideas, and voice that made this a story worth telling and a book worth writing. Yaram Yahu, your work as our cultural sensitivity editor both encouraged us and emboldened us to add more in the way of texture, setting, and sense of place, and improved this work in vast and sweeping ways.

It feels impossible to name all of the folks at Morgan James, our publisher, who played a role in some form or another along the way: Jill, David, Isaiah, Lisa, our cover design team, our mastermind team, and any others I am surely missing, thank you for taking a chance on this story. In a time where the testimonies of refugees, immigrants, and all those deemed "other" in American culture are increasingly marginalized, demeaned, and overlooked, your willingness to embrace and promote this story is a testament to the integrity of your company. I am so glad to be a part of the Morgan James team!

And to you, dear reader, who chooses to read this story. To open a book is to open yourself: to learning, to growth, to challenge, to questions, to answers, to wonder, to beauty. In a time where such things are resisted, or under-appreciated, your support of an author and a story like this is nothing short of a radical resistance against a culture which is so often reducible down to polarization, pragmatism, and stagnancy. May you find in these pages something that, in some way, changes you.

This book is based on true events from the life of Bikonzi Moise and his family. Some names, characters, and descriptions have been altered for privacy reasons, and in some cases, composite characters have been developed to represent true events.

CHAPTER 1:
TAKEN

"When two elephants fight, it is the grass that gets hurt."
-African Proverb

Evening settled upon the land of Mbuji-Mayi. A mist hung in the air, a laundry line of moisture cast from tree to tree. A warm heaviness presided over surrounding structures and shrubs alike and hooded by the dark, leafy shadows of the trees that loomed over the dim soil. A thin sliver of the silver crescent moon peeked its way through those silent canopies, accented by the cacophony of nameless insects who soundtracked the dark. Assorted trash, kicked up only hours earlier, was scattered aimlessly, mixed together with dust, and unmoving. This ordinarily busy city, the third largest in the Democratic Republic of the Congo, now simply sat as if in anticipation. It was viciously still, violently static.

The streets spoke silent stories—of the destruction of infrastructure, of class conflict, of power jockeying—into the night air. It was breathed daily, the oxygen of the Hutus and the Tutsis. Tribe opposed tribe, and neighbor opposed neighbor. A divisive cultural virus, foreign to these lands and brought by Western judgments and powers, permeated every level of life, and this left many in the city to live in a perpetual state of looking over their shoulders. For centuries, the peoples of Congo lived alongside one another, and their differences were named, understood, and navigated when present. But when alternate eyes saw this place primarily for what could be extracted from it and saw its people as means to their own ends, the language of hierarchies and inequalities soaked the ground as much as its persistent rains. Darting eyes, careful steps, and hidden lives were all regular productions, consistent expressions of vigilant fear made requisite by ungodly persecution. The language one spoke—from Lingala to Swahili to Tshiluba—or the area in which one lived, or the bridge of one's nose could all warrant death and violence now. Each man, each family, and each group remained in a state of constant self-awareness, for their reputation or interactions could have devastating results on their future. Dread hovered over the city, a swarm of bees over water, primed to strike upon any breaking of the surface.

Most homes were largely simplistic and of similar size, placed upon small plots of land and spaced little from one another. Though there existed defined neighborhoods, consistencies in street structure were lacking, as many dead-ended into small clusters of trees, or were otherwise abruptly cut off. All travel remained difficult; roads were undefined or poorly organized, and this trend continued as one moved away from the central city and into local farms.

The Moise family home stood prominently in its place, unique both in its larger size and structure from those nearby. A five-foot tall fence surrounded it on all sides. Concrete floors filled the place, contrasting the dirt found in neighboring homes. Even artistic tiles, divided into black and white halves diagonally, covered their main hallway, from the living room to the bedrooms. A patio surrounded the front door. Anyone who approached it rightly was family, regardless of blood relation; friends and neighbors were invited regularly. This night, however, as had been the case in many recent weeks, it was stagnant. It creaked with a usual progression, moved by time and weather, but it seemed unused, a ghost house where a former home had resided. The windows were shut, and the door locked.

Bikonzi—called B by those near to him—sat inside with each of his six siblings, the six-year-old middle son. A collection of dishes was spread across their table: plantains, fried and soft, complemented a single large pot of stew filled with rice, tomatoes, pumpkin, onion, cassava, a few pieces of salted and spiced bushmeat, and chili peppers. A plate full of dozens of pieces of fufu sat just adjacent, waiting to be dipped into the stew and to soak in its flavor. Their table was an image of the joy and bounty of the land they called home. Yet the Moises did not sit there; they instead huddled close together, crouched in their main room with their heads bowed and eyes tightly squeezed shut. Two small candles remained their only illumination.

"Papá, Nzambe," prayed Rose, Bikonzi's mother, in Lingala, one of the many local languages in which she was versed.

The family's small, short tears shot through the room, but the words continued on.

"Give us strength to forgive one another."

B, reverently still aware of the moment, kept his head slightly bowed but allowed his mind and eyes to wander. He peripherally scanned the room, taking in his siblings all crouched around him, their arms creating an encompassing fence. He peeked at his father, who sat with them that night and noted his expression. It was one of holding tightly, strained faces and pursed lips containing something of this moment. The entirety of a soul could be found on that face. It was one B had not quite seen before. It was as if he were discovering a new land on a map, somehow overlooked or hidden in previous encounters. He grasped his hands more tightly to his sister and brother, to his right and left, respectively, in imitation.

"We do not know what is to come. We do not know what might happen."

B now shifted focus to his pajamas. He never truly needed more than what he and his brothers wore tonight: raffia shorts and a cotton shirt provided the warmth and comfort of home for him. Both of his parents retained their more colorful attire, as they often did, even into the late hours of the night: his mother donned a yellow and pink liputa dress, her hair bound tightly in a matching headdress, and his father wore his usual dashiki style shirt, long and maroon, with spinning patterns of white threaded around his neck. In spite of their large family size, they always had enough for everyone, whether in food or clothing.

"Let us forgive one another."

B's attention was suddenly diverted to a faint voice coming from outside their walls. It initially sounded like his neighbor and family friend, Traya, though it was too muffled for him to say with certainty. He perked his ears and strained to listen, his distraction from the prayer now firmly in place. More voices could be heard, this time louder and nearer, though still muffled.

"Let us forgive."

The voices grew louder, and B could now clearly hear Traya. She had urgency in her tone but not in warning—it was almost as if she was seeking them out. Tears from inside the room muffled her, and more male voices from beyond their walls drowned her out, speaking directly but authoritatively to her and to one another, though he could not make out their words. It sounded as if there were three or four men in all.

"Webale, Nzambe."

A sudden obstructive bang against the door startled B and forced his head to look to the entrance to the house.

"Amen."

That was when the door was broken in.

Abrupt banging and yelling filled the house. Crying joined in from both inside and outside, a chaotic chorus of confusion and conflict. Armed soldiers stormed in. Weapons and strength brought new authority. Rose finished with her prayer and, in the midst of the frenzied situation, grabbed her husband and uttered one word.

"Run."

Bikonzi's father fled the room swiftly, and the boy quickly lost sight of him amidst the hectic haze and blackness. Government officials had come numerous times to their home searching for him in recent weeks; Bikonzi would notice them through the cracked door answered by his mother. She'd tell them that his father was absent each time, that some work venture had him traveling or working away from home, and her words were mostly true. Whether or not it was because of his work, Bikonzi's father had in many ways become like a ghost, gone for days at a time and arriving at home often under the cover of darkness through their back door. He ate meals and prayed in quiet with them, hardly speaking, and when he did, in deep, hushed words. Then, after a couple of days of this, he'd disappear before the sun rose one morning, gone for two or three more days before restarting the same cycle.

He remembered asking his mother about this on a couple of occasions. She'd always say, "Your father's working…he's working. So that we can be taken care of. So that we can be happy. And safe..." Her voice would trail off then, and her eyes would start to water. He certainly had not felt safe on the instances the soldiers had come to their door in the past, looking for his father. And it seemed they had finally timed their arrival rightly, guided by Traya, who now stood a few feet inside the door, observing the calamity with a calm, thinking expression cast across her face, almost directing the action that played out in front of her, as if to say, *If I'm going, they're going with me*.

The family was ordered through the front doorway and into a truck that awaited them outside. Vitriolic condemnations filled the night air.

"Cockroaches!"

The word rang through the rooms of the home, conjuring in Bikonzi's mind the scuttering image of those vile insects. He never hesitated when he glimpsed them intruding upon the kitchen or his bedroom; he'd jump to his feet and stomp them to mush whenever he got the chance. They were disgusting in his eyes. Savagely, the soldiers shoved each of them out and told them to leave everything but the clothes they wore.

With the momentary vision of his father's flight from the room, Bikonzi felt the pull to follow. Glimpsing back to the door, where he watched his family being jostled out to the truck, he shifted his focus to the hall. Fleeting thoughts fluttered through him as he took in his family's state. Images filled his mind and flew through in half-seconds: his sisters crying, his mother ushering them out the door with her hands on their heads, his father wasting no time in running, his older brothers resisting. By the time these thoughts had concluded, and his own tears had subsided enough for him to see clearly, he realized he did not know where his father had fled. There was no sign of him now near the back of the house, and B—still understanding the urgency of the moment—quickly dashed out of sight.

Safety beckoned him into his parent's bedroom. He threw himself to the floor and rolled under their bed. The voices were distant again, separated by walls and more warm air. B slowed his breathing, swallowing his rapidly beating heart and focusing his ears on the other room. More yelling. "Cockroaches!" the Hutu invaders repeated again. Those words began to fade as well, and B could hear footsteps exiting the house. He no longer heard the voices of his family; the yelling of his older brothers, John and Moses, had quieted; the tears of his older sister, Amiee, were gone from the house; his mother and his younger siblings, Jay, Seth, and Team, had dissolved. A roaring silence fell over the house.

A brief calm embraced him. He heard his own breathing, his own heart. He let his face fall to the ground, closing his eyes. Silent tears still fell, wetting the floor his head rested on. Yet deafening, wordless thoughts abruptly intruded. He thought about his family, his father, his life. If he remained here, what would happen to them? Where would *he* go? He had heard stories of family separation, of death camps, from his friends. He had thought they were only rumors and that even if they were true, they were out *there* in the world somewhere. That wouldn't happen to a family who went to church, who prayed, who was good. Death was just a rumored antagonist, far away from his own life. That story couldn't be his story.

His thoughts quickly shifted back to his family. His parents and siblings were all he knew, all he had ever known, and all he lived for. Though he felt God might be with him, how was he to know God without family? Where was God underneath this bed? Where was God in the dark heat of night? Bikonzi was utterly alone.

And, whether out of reflex, love, or simply the consideration of his life, he yelled.

"Mom!"

No response.

"Mom!"

Footsteps moved quickly back into the house.

"Mom!"

Bikonzi was swept out from under the shield of the bed, grabbed tightly, and pulled back through his house. They dragged him through the front door, though he—for the avoidance of additional pain—resisted little. Tears fell as his only defense. Looking back through the door frame, he saw the dinner table, food scattered across its face and onto the floor. He saw the familiar furniture: the wooden chairs and couch, carved with designs telling the stories of some unknown family eating together, and the long, thick wooden table, supported by legs carved into the shape of elephants. He could almost feel the worn texture of that wood. It felt like home.

He was thrown onto the truck bed, now filled with four families. His mother embraced him and gathered him in with her children. The key turned in the ignition, and the truck began to roll away.

In looking back to his house as they drove, he noticed in the dim light only the mangled fence.

He felt a slight breeze on his bare arms.

The darkness of the night had broken it, pressing on his mind.

CHAPTER 2:
COCKROACHES

"The axe forgets but the tree remembers."
-African Proverb

The bed of the truck bounced as it hit a bump in the rough road, jumping Bikonzi from his sleep and mother's grasp momentarily. This brought his eyes away from their safety and into his surroundings. His family sat tightly together in one corner of the truck bed, fatherless and cold. Those younger than him fastened shut their eyes in fear and confusion while his elder siblings stared mildly, a dark solemnity firmly settled into their expressions. He darted his sight to the others in the truck, outlines and eyes faintly visible in the dark: three additional families huddled together within themselves, each in their own corner, displaying an increasingly loud inner distress in their silence. They took the form of concerned eyes, staring distantly into the black nothing of the night, eyebrows angling in unsure fear, and lips turned down in concerned anger and sadness.

After what felt like an hour since they had been taken, there was little else for B to do than rest. His mind was scattered, a mess of confusion and disarray, and it kept him from being able to focus. He tried to recollect the sensory observations of the last hour, seeking to recall the sounds, the smells, and the sights that he had taken in, but much of it remained a blur. Clamoring voices of confusion and chaos rang in his mind while the smell of his family's stew called to his now grumbling stomach. These reflections kept him in a steady state of blankness, conscious of the world but constrained by his own mental mess, his brain the back of an expansive tapestry. Thoughts of his clothes, his food, his home, his family, his father, his God—all swirled enough to recognize, yet dissipated quickly enough to keep him from clarity.

He began to perspire, and it was in this mental and physical space, enveloped by darkness and in silence of speech, that he first really felt it. It had certainly crept into his thoughts before, but mostly in sleep and distant daydreams. It had never been more real, more known than in this moment. Death—a looming presence, a shadowy figure stalking the corners of his mind—took central place there now, sinking into his psyche. Like feet in tar, it stuck, beginning its encompassing of his mind in methodical, experienced, intentional movement. He sank back into his mother's chest, eyes now firmly open.

It was then the truck jerked to an abrupt stop.

Just as violently as they were cast into the truck only an hour earlier, they were now thrust out into the night. Guns were aimed haphazardly in their direction in the unloading process. The littlest ones clung tightly to their mothers, whimpering softly. An amplified sobbing was only prevented by the sheer intimidation of the oppressors at hand. More curses rang through the quiet air, electric verbal jabs urging them along.

Bikonzi exited the truck next to his brother Moses, both of them following immediately behind their mother. She led their family with her head aimed toward the dirt, prompting the same action in her children. They walked to a simple, one-story building faded from a formerly vibrant yellow. A thick metal door remained as the main entrance into a lobby area, though the building expanded on both sides. An open-door frame at the back of this lobby revealed a wooden post behind the building, around ten feet tall, staked into the ground.

Each family was led in, staying tightly together, walking through the main door two by two, as its width allowed. Upon entering, they stepped into the lobby, which expanded into corridors on both the right and left, a hallway into the reaches of the rest of the structure. Bikonzi noted the scarcity of light in the place. Flickering bulbs lined the hallway, set a few yards apart from one another. Dampness hovered there, and he heard the faint and inconsistent dripping of water.

They were the second family to enter, following Traya. Amidst the dim light, B noticed a guard and accompanying desk facing the entry door for the first time. Poking his head out of the mob of his siblings—who remained tightly bound together, as if connected by string—Bikonzi now noticed his cousin, Daniel, clinging to the back of the mob and attempting to stay hidden behind them. B didn't see Daniel's family anywhere.

"How old is he?!"

The guard sitting behind the desk abruptly spoke, breaking into Bikonzi's thoughts. He pointed through the family to Daniel directly, his voice echoing in the sparse and hollow building.

Rose said nothing. The rest of the room mirrored her silence. She moved her eyes to meet his, keeping her head tilted slightly downward.

Immediately after their eyes met, the guard sprung up from his chair, grabbing a previously hidden AK-47 in one motion. He aimed it at Daniel.

"Take him!"

Without hesitation, two fellow soldiers standing in the dark corners of the room swarmed around Daniel, each grabbing an arm. He resisted aggressively, squirming in an attempt to free himself from their grasp. The butt of the gun landed swiftly into his lower back, causing him to yelp and grimace in pain.

Bikonzi had heard that yelp before. He and Daniel grew up living next to one another, and they always referred to one another as cousins, though they were of no blood relation. Their proximity made them particularly close, and in this moment he was brought back to the playground only a few months earlier. He played soccer alongside his brothers, cousins, and neighbors in their usual physical and competitive spirit. John and Moses would often have their way, their size and strength enabling them to muscle their way to the ball and, in some cases, even cast aside the other boys with a clever, if not subtle, occasional elbow. After a powerful kick soared to the goal, flipping the field and nearing a score, Daniel leaped into the air adjacent to John—a full four years the junior of the 16-year-old—and attempted a header. John's strength overpowered him, pushing him to the ground unintentionally. His back bent awkwardly as he landed, and a grimace and yelp emerged involuntarily as he crumpled down. The game paused as many of the boys ran to Daniel's side, but before they could surround him too tightly, he jumped from the ground and emerged through the building crowd, limping and muttering, "I'm fine. I'm fine."

Bikonzi knew Daniel as fiery and tough, so it didn't surprise him now that he resisted so strongly the brute force of these soldiers. It filled him at once with fear and anger to see such an unfair disparity in strength, to see his fierce friend forced upon him in such a way. His face and chest grew warm as the soldiers forced Daniel out of the room, leading him through an open doorway toward one of the cells on the left side of the building. He was left with a great tension: a part of him wanted to chase after Daniel, using that rising heat of anger to throw his arms and legs feverishly into those abusers and free his cousin. He stayed back, though, recognizing that if they could handle Daniel with such relative ease, his added resistance wouldn't make much of a difference.

Looking around at each of the families who had entered the building, he realized there were no men present, and pieced together from their taking of Daniel, they must be removing all the older boys and men along the way. They were ensuring there was no one strong enough to fight back. He wondered what his father would do if he were here. He wished he was larger, stronger like his father; he remembered his muscled forearms, forged from his decades-long guitar-playing, and his booming voice that carried for what seemed like miles to him. Yet even his father seemed powerless to resist the night before: he was a musician, a churchman, hardly a match for machine guns. Bikonzi had never felt such a desire to fight back paired with such helplessness.

After watching Daniel's forced exit unfold, Rose returned her eyes to the ground in front of her, and her children clung more tightly together, with John and Moses masked in the center. Bikonzi noticed John glance quickly at Moses before fading into the mass of people and lowering his head slightly. John was older, and Moses was only slightly younger than Daniel, and they seemed fully aware that they were as much at risk of being taken away themselves. Perhaps it was boys twelve years or older who they demanded be separated, Bikonzi wondered to himself. The guard who had yelled returned to his seat.

"How many of you?" the soldier behind the desk demanded of Rose. His gun remained set across his lap as he spoke.

"Eight. Myself and seven children."

"How old is your oldest?" he asked.

"Eleven."

He paused and examined her with a cold stare before resuming.

"Where is your husband?" he continued, not breaking his gaze from her face.

"I don't know."

He was silent, unblinking. Rose stood before him, covering herself with one arm while shielding her children with the other. B felt as if this silence lasted an hour. Clamoring families could be heard behind them. The air was filled only by spurts of tears.

"Take them away," the soldier broke through the stillness, motioning his hand as if swatting a bug.

Two guards, having just returned from removing Daniel, now spurred the Moises along the same hallway. Their weapons were staffs, herding the sheep forward under scattered light and amidst damp darkness. They smelled of sweat and soil, their faces solemn and unflinching.

Bikonzi kept his head facing downward as they walked but darted his eyes to his left as they were shuffled together. Immediately after leaving the main lobby, they were led past a small cell with walls on three sides and bars covering the front. He caught a glimpse of a few teenage boys inside, scattered throughout the space and lying around. Some of them looked asleep, while others stirred little. Each of them was bloody, covered by tattered clothes stained deep red and black. He could not tell if Daniel was present amongst them. One peered up just as Bikonzi walked past, his eyes red and weak.

The hallway continued to what appeared to be similar cells, three or four beyond the first room. The Moises were shoved into one of the cells, the one just adjacent to the first they had passed, and the barred door abruptly slammed behind them. A small puddle in the middle filled a large abrasion in the concrete floor. The walls were solid on three sides, and there was no window allowing any glimpses beyond the building.

Sleep that night came in fits. For B, it was the first time he had ever slept outside of his own home. The floor was cold and hard. The air was dense, like breathing soup. His stomach perpetually growled. He regretted not grabbing a few handfuls of fufu during the commotion of the evening before and attempting to stash it in his pockets.

During the few times he was able to drift away, he was always awakened by noises from the cell next door. Yells, cries, and agony rang through the shared wall. He heard thuds against the ground and loud, sharp, smacking sounds. Steady moaning floated through to his ears. He had never heard the voice of pain so clearly, so constantly, than in that evening. The sounds narrated his dreams, making it difficult to discern what was real and what was the nightmare of his unconscious imagination.

It was during this half-sleep state, in between dreams, that it happened. At least, it seemed to have happened: B glimpsed what he believed to be his father. A man of similar stature and dressed in a white shirt like the one he had last seen his father wearing walked down the hallway, hands in cuffs, head down, escorted by two armed men. B's eyes squinted in disbelief as he lay down. His vision was fuzzy. And before he had a chance to jump up, before he could call out for him, he had disappeared past the cell and down the hallway. If he had been there at all, he was gone just as abruptly.

The next two days were filled with static and forced routine. The family was provided a cup of rice and water in the mornings, oftentimes tossed into the cell. They split this between them, leaving a few grains for each. Some of them saved their portion to be eaten throughout the day. B chose to eat all of his as soon as he had received it. More families were shoved down the hallway into adjacent cells, often meant to house only two or three inmates. Many of the abusive noises continued throughout the day, a soundtrack to Bikonzi's limited perspective.

During the second evening, a soldier approached the cell, staring down at the family through the bars. He stood unmoving briefly before shouting.

"You! Cockroach!"

Rose stood in response.

"Come with me."

She turned and stared quickly at each of her children, who gazed back, pleading with her not to leave. With eyes that housed a thousand words, she spoke none. Her glimpse alone assured her return. She was led out of Bikonzi's sight, and the siblings all shared stoic, unspeaking looks with one another. Many of them looked down or around the room. B observed all of this, and he proceeded to look down into the puddle in the middle of their cell, which had grown slightly since their arrival. It was muddy, reflecting back the bare concrete ceiling, a brown and unclean mirror.

After an enduring thirty minutes, Rose returned. Her children surrounded her and hugged her, tears narrating their embrace.

"Move!" commanded the soldier who had escorted her back, aiming his gun in their direction. She quickly released her embrace and uttered to her children, "Come. Stay near me."

They were forced back down the hallway, and as they passed through the lobby, B managed to glimpse through the open doorway at the back of the room. He saw the wooden post again, illuminated by a dim yellow light. This time, there was a man attached to it. His face was buried in the wood, exposing only his bare back. Lashes were evident all over, zigging, zagging, and overlapping in deep, red lines. His hands were bound together with a rope, which was strung from the top of the post above his head. His legs appeared unable to hold his body up; only the rope supported him and kept him upright. Bikonzi turned back to the front entrance, following his family through the doorway and into the harsh and thick night.

The same military truck that had transported them to the jail facility awaited them again now, already running and spewing out exhaust into the dark. The dense gas, combined with the night's humidity, stung Bikonzi's nostrils. He coughed and grimaced as his family was corralled into the bed again. Three other families followed, each recognizable to Bikonzi, though he didn't know all of them equally well. They each filed to different designated corners, heads down and feet dragging. After the bed of the truck was filled, the tailgate was abruptly shut, and the soldier who forced them in slammed the tailgate two times. They jolted to a start.

Suddenly, just as the truck began to move, B noticed two hands grasp tightly onto the back of the bed. He quickly tapped Moses's arm, silently pointing. As the speed increased, the hands came into clearer focus: they were connected to arms, then to a torso, and then to an entire body. After some effort, a boy fell limply into the bed.

At first, Bikonzi had trouble recognizing him. Collapsing, the boy simply laid down, his back to the Moise family. He breathed short, shallow breaths, his entire body expanding and contracting as he did. Bikonzi noticed first the red stripes across his back: they were fresh, some of them still dripping blood. It reminded him of a zebra. He could hardly tell what was striped and what was solid. He wore only a pair of ragged shorts covered in a mixture of dirt and sweat. His face began to turn, and B still squinted in an effort to see him in the pale moonlight. One of his front teeth was missing, and he spat blood from his mouth. His face looked swollen, and dried blood rested on the bridge of his upper lip. His right eye was dark and squinted. It was only after some seconds of staring, and amidst his own horror, that Bikonzi realized the identity of the human in front of him, gulping dryly as he did. It was Daniel.

CHAPTER 3:
HOLES

"He who digs a grave for his enemy might as well be digging one for himself."
-African Proverb

Rose sprung up from her corner and embraced the boy, gingerly placing her hands around him. Though he wrapped himself around her in response, he did not cry. Bikonzi glimpsed briefly an emptiness in his eyes before he shut them from exhaustion. It was a stare that had seen more than it should. The outlines of his ribs were visible against his black and red skin, and he gladly welcomed the strength of another to carry him across the truck bed, resting in Rose's arms.

No one spoke as the truck continued bounding forward. Moses scrunched his body together and turned to close his eyes. John stood tall on his knees just behind Rose, eyes vigilant. Amiee sat nearest the little ones, arms wrapped around each of them.

Bikonzi could barely discern voices from inside the truck cab against the backdrop of the rattling drive.

"We should just kill them now," one soldier started. "There's no point in feeding and housing them anyways. It's a waste of resources."

"Our orders were clear," the other soldier rebutted.

"Forget orders – who will miss these ones? Why would we take them to be killed when we could just get rid of them here?"

A long silence between them followed.

Suddenly, the truck jolted to a stop, throwing the women and children around haphazardly. The two men rushed out of the cab, ripping open the tailgate and aiming their weapons toward Bikonzi, his family, and the rest of the families.

"Move!"

One word, coupled with the wrong end of two guns, communicated clearly enough. They all began to shuffle out of the truck bed. They were led to the side of the road, forced to their knees, and lined shoulder to shoulder. Bikonzi was aligned at the end of his family. He watched the rest of the women and children file out, some crying, some simply solemn. The soldiers directed, poking and prodding with their weapons. As they did, a voice broke into the chaos, sudden and subdued.

"I saw an angel," it said.

Bikonzi quickly scanned amongst those still exiting the truck. None of them seemed to be speaking.

"An angel spoke to me," it continued.

It was then Bikonzi realized the voice was coming from a figure down the line from him, already on their knees. He leaned forward slightly and noticed Christian urgently but discreetly looking amongst his family and neighbors. He had the attention of the entire line while the soldiers were still distracted by forcing the others out of the truck.

Christian and his family had lived close to the Moises growing up, and from what Bikonzi could tell, they were also taken in the middle of the night, as each of them was clothed in pajamas. Christian had an older brother, David, who knelt beside him, his face turning to Christian in confusion and anger. The family continued down the line: their younger sister, Ana, and two other younger brothers, one of whom–Abel–was a baby, not more than a couple of months old. Christian's mother, Eden, held Abel tightly, wrapping him in what looked like torn bed sheets. She, too, turned as Christian spoke, shooshing him quietly with a face full of fear, her nostrils flared and eyes wide. Her efforts did not deter her son from continuing.

"He was wearing white. He told me that most of us will suffer, but only a few of us will die. Most of us will make it."

That was the conclusion of his insight. His mother reservedly smiled, pulling his head close and quieting him. Bikonzi leaned back and faced the ground, turning his head slightly as he considered the words. He had never seen an angel before, let alone heard a word from one. He remembered being told stories by his family when this had happened to people—the angel appearing to Mary to inform her of Jesus's arrival, angels appearing to people like Saul or John—but they had always been just that: stories. He was initially angry: how could Christian say something hopeful when Death was so near and inevitable? Did he really think he was helping everyone else with those comments? Bikonzi felt an urge to walk over and shut him up himself, but he refrained, given the soldiers and guns. He just kept spinning his words over in his head. It felt stupid and reckless, yet clear; it was wild, yet strong. As each moment passed, Bikonzi felt a faint hope rise up alongside his anger. He hoped Christian was right. He hoped they would make it.

The rest of the truck had been lined up now, and the soldiers stood in front of them, taking in their work. They muttered under their breath again to one another.

"They're here, they're lined up. Let's just kill them now."

Any flicker of hope that had arisen in Bikonzi's heart with Christian's comments was dashed to pieces. Death had taken over his mind once more.

"That would be easiest for us..."

"That's what I mean—we could be praised for our efficiency."

"We could be... what if the general wants them to be delivered for him to kill, though? Our orders were to *deliver* them."

As they continued, the men started to turn increasingly toward one another and away from the families. Bikonzi dared not lift his gaze to watch their bickering.

"Our orders were to deliver them so they could be killed. We are removing an extra step and saving time."

"True. But what if we've got the wrong people? They're speaking our language; how do we know this is who they want?"

"Look at their noses! Their eyes! You can tell it just by looking at them, by smelling them. They're not ours."

Their voices were becoming louder now, and their arguments were increasingly muddied. Bikonzi ran his finger down his nose slowly, following its contours and shape and wondering why these men were so concerned with it.

"But they are speaking our language. How can you know..."

"Are you scared?! What's the worst that could happen if we get rid of them now?"

The soldiers were shouting at one another now.

"They're willing to kill *them*! They may be willing to kill *us*!"

"If you won't do this, then I will!"

They started to shove and pound one another's chests, their violence rerouted, and their conversation fully distracted. This continued for a few moments before they stopped, staring wide-eyed in anger at one another.

"Do what you want. I can tell them this was your idea and that I had no part in it."

Silence followed for a few moments. Then one of the men finally—seemingly out of frustration more than anything else—simply exclaimed: "Crawl back into the truck, roaches!"

Everyone swiftly scurried back, and within minutes, the truck continued on its way. Two other guards were picked up shortly afterward to accompany Bikonzi, his family, and the other families on their drive, armed with machetes to prevent any escape attempts. They climbed into the back of the truck, and B made sure to avoid eye contact with either of them. He sat on his own, his back leaning against the cab side of the truck bed. He wondered what angels looked like.

They arrived at the facility early in the morning. They had come upon it abruptly, as seemingly endless miles of jungle suddenly gave way to an open clearing of dirt and scattered buildings. With visibility only out of the back of the truck, B initially saw the layout of the place in spurts as buildings appeared part-way in view. They rode in on a loose dirt road, hardly distinguishable from the expanse of emptiness around it. Only a few dozen feet from the tree line and entrance to the camp, on the left of the road from where Bikonzi sat, stood a large, empty two-story warehouse. Though it had window frames, much of the glass was broken or damaged, leaving only square holes places scattered throughout walls of decaying paint.

Before he could see much else, the truck abruptly rolled to a stop, at which point the guards slammed their doors and stepped noisily and aggressively on the soft and muddy ground. They had driven through the night, and the intensity of the morning sun assaulted Bikonzi's eyes. He squinted uncomfortably as the guards circled to the back of the truck again and forced each family out onto the soft and muddy ground into a disorganized mob of bodies. Each family huddled together, attempting to hide the youngest and most vulnerable behind their mothers.

It was only after they were all kneeling on the ground and his eyes were adjusted to the light that Bikonzi was able to fully grasp his surroundings. Scattered nearby at varying distances were an abundance of tan office buildings, each with different military vehicles parked outside. In the distance in each direction was a thick jungle. No fence surrounded the place, but it was easy now for B to understand why: the families were crouched before a crowd of around two dozen soldiers. He couldn't see all of them in the crowd, and he dared not stare at them long enough to count. They varied in age from teenagers to middle-aged men, all dressed in combat green and tan. Each of them was armed, many with multiple weapons, and they now stood menacingly over the crouched group. They were adorned with varying helmets and hats, some metal and some fabric, each of them jungle green. Their uniforms expanded into other camouflage shades of light and dark green, and each of them often carried a flash of uniqueness: a personal pin here, a necklace there. Yet their unique flourishes did not strip away their unspoken and aligned intent at destruction: B could feel it through their piercing stares. Though he had not yet considered an escape attempt at this point, it was clear now that the thought of such an action was futile in the face of these boys and men. Any amount of power he held was at their mercy. B, in step with the rest of his family, avoided direct eye contact by staring down to the ground.

After a minute or so of silence, two specific figures emerged from the military crowd, drawing Bikonzi to glimpse slightly upward to see them. One was a broad-shouldered, tall, bald man adorned in a beret-style hat with three stars spaced across the front and a camouflage uniform. The second was thinner, though still tall; perhaps they appeared that way from Bikonzi's knees. They both donned garb that appeared more official than the scattered men behind them.

The first man held his hands tightly behind his back and began to pace in front of them, each step squelching slightly into the mud and rocks, the ground giving way to his heavy boots. He wore sunglasses, preventing Bikonzi from seeing his eyes, but he never broke his gaze from the families in front of him. The second man did not pace but simply stood, squinting and looking the group over. His eyebrows tilted down as if those in front of him were a nuisance, an infringement upon the world he believed should exist. His mouth showed no expression, a straight line across his long face. He had sunken cheeks, and his chin jutted notably out from the rest of his profile. After looking them over, he began to speak.

"I am Commander Andre. This is Commander Gelor. Who are you?" he bellowed authoritatively.

The only sound of response was a gust of wind blowing up a cloud of dust nearby. B bounced his eyes around the crowd, noticing some to be shaking.

"Who are you?!" He increased his volume this time, pointing his index finger toward the mass of bodies in front of him.

B saw the veins of his neck bulging, his head glistening as sweat began to gather upon his face.

"*Who are you?!*" He now shouted, his voice carrying to the tree line in the distance, right foot stomping into the dirt as he did. The first man continued to pace calmly, like a lion inspecting for the opportune moment to strike.

The silence continued again for a few lonely seconds when suddenly a familiar voice broke through. Without raising her head, Rose spoke quietly and steadily.

"Commanders, you know all of us. You stole us away from our homes. Why do you ask this?"

B inched closer to his mother after she said these things, following the examples of John and Moses; if either man were to jump toward her, they would have to deal with these brothers first. Bikonzi reasoned it would not make much difference.

Commander Andre simply stood stoically above them, shoulders back and hands now folded behind him. He did not speak, and his head now blocked out the sun, preventing B from seeing his response. His face was now only a dark outline before them. No one spoke or moved.

Suddenly, a subtle laugh broke out. It was a low chuckle from a dry throat, bleeding out from the shadow of the man in front of them. It was joined by Commander Gelor, whose eyes turned down to the dirt as he paced. A quick motion was made to the crowd of soldiers behind them.

Another man approached the standing commander and handed him a clipboard.

"These are their names, sir," he said. The commander began to scan the list in front of him, pacing again as he did. After reading the list, he stopped again and spoke directly.

"Bring the shovels."

Four men emerged from the mass of guards, each with their arms full. They scurried forward, tossing them between him and the still kneeling and shaking families. Bikonzi noticed a few of the soldiers begin to smile and laugh amongst one another as this happened.

"You will be digging," the thin man began, "It does not matter to me who digs, only that the holes are finished. One hole for each family. Make sure it is large enough for all of you."

He then turned his back on them and walked a few yards behind his men toward the office building. The soldiers scattered, some following the commander and others dispersing toward the other buildings spread across the base. They left the families alone.

The first to grab a shovel was John. He rose quietly, grabbed the splintered wooden tool, spaced himself away from the other families, and went to work on the hard ground. Bikonzi heard other children begin to cry, asking why they needed to dig. Moses joined John, grabbing an additional shovel. They worked under the sun for an hour. They spoke of how heavy and difficult the ground was to displace at first but eventually gave us their complaints—each breaking of dirt simply became less productive as they went, their bodies weakened without food and sun-dried. It was then that Bikonzi was revisited by that creeping darkness he had only just met a few nights before. He stared blankly into the dirt as his brothers moved it, the hole growing steadily deeper and darker. Death was a hole this time, black and shallow, as clear as the one that grew before his eyes. It caused a shudder over him, which then quickly gave way to a numbing of his body. Hunger and thirst disappeared. His vision narrowed around the edges, focused narrowly upon the relocation of the earth in front of him. He thought about each shovel of dirt abruptly gathered and moved to a pile on the surface. It did not choose; it did not respond. It was at the mercy of forces well beyond its control. He tried to think about God but could not find him in the dirt.

As each family neared completion of their digging, four more soldiers returned, guns strapped around their chests as they approached. They split themselves and surrounded the group, with two moving behind them and two more directing from the front. One yelled for the group to rise and walk, and their progress was slow and weak. This caused the two soldiers at the back of the group to begin shoving and kicking the children nearest them. Bikonzi turned and glimpsed the mother of his good friend Fistan, pleading for them to stop kicking her son, and he saw the butt of a gun promptly lowered into her head. Bikonzi closed his eyes and flinched, reacting as if his was the face being assaulted. An exhausted sadness fell over him, and he slowly reopened his eyes to see her. She arose bloodied and silent, tears streaming down her face as she kept walking.

The group was moved toward the large, seemingly deserted warehouse he had seen near the entrance. They were funneled through a doorless opening on the north side into a dirty, open space; this was the only way into and out of the space. The concrete floors were cracked and indented, lacking consistency throughout. There were no dividing walls in the place, no designated rooms, and only one large area, which Bikonzi estimated was about 50 feet in each direction. Though it provided them much more room than their cell in the prior jail, it hardly alleviated the Bikonzi's anxiety, being this far from home and unsure of what was to come next. The families were shoved in hastily, and they began to gather amongst themselves, each separating to a different corner.

Bikonzi and his family took the corner nearest the doorway they entered through on the north side of the warehouse, the soldiers standing and staring over them as they did. The other three families grouped themselves around the three other corners. B looked around and saw little movement; most of the children lay on the concrete, withered, exhausted, and dirty. He attempted to do the same, but he was unable to find even space upon which to lie. He placed his left hip into a gap in the concrete, and his upper body extended onto the cold floor. He noticed that his knees were beginning to crack and bleed, and the strength of his thirst returned to him. He closed his eyes, glad to be rid of the images around him, even if only for a short time.

After a few hours of residing here, more men arrived in the large room. B thought it to be late afternoon at this point, as the sky was beginning to fill with more color and the sun was falling to the ground. With few words, the soldiers again gathered the families up and led them out of the room and across the base on foot. They arose with more haste this time, remembering the abuse that prompted them to the building before.

It seemed that many had been able to capture fits of sleep as well, even amidst the uneven and bare floor, and this may have helped with providing increased energy.

The Moise family was the first to exit, followed by the other three groups. As they walked, Bikonzi saw a photograph hanging from the belt of one of the soldiers; the corners were withered and it was largely faded. He could not make it out completely, but he noticed numerous faces present and smiling.

They were led out to the jungle, away from the other buildings in the camp. They had walked for a few minutes before reaching the tree line and were now prompted to climb their way through short bushes and around trees. After about five minutes, the sound of quiet, running water filled Bikonzi's ears. He was immediately reminded again of the dryness of his mouth, and each of his senses perked at the potential of tasting water for the first time today.

The stream arose suddenly in their midst. It was not more than three feet wide, and though it moved slightly, the water was brown and unclear. It snaked through the trees and, in either direction, was lost after only a few dozen yards into the density of the jungle. The soldiers directed them all to undress and bathe as their smell wafted to the residences of some of the commanding officers at the camp, disgusting them. They were also told to drink, as this was the closest and only water source for miles.

Bikonzi approached the water with his family and collapsed onto his hands and knees, bringing his head down and drinking directly from the stream. He could taste small pockets of dirt in each mouthful, yet he drank freely; nothing would prevent him from watering his mouth and bringing life to his body. He drank like this for a few minutes, stopping occasionally to catch his breath before returning. After quenching himself, he plopped down next to the stream, wiping his mouth and resting. His belly was full; he could feel the water sloshing around. He looked up and around the stream, noticing the life that clung to this source of water. Spiders danced between bushes, building webs to sustain themselves. Ants crawled near the water and through the mud around it. He heard crickets chirping nearby, always unseen yet perpetually heard and alive with music. Even the trees leaned forward, creating a green canopy, their roots jockeying for position amidst one another. He then turned his attention to the other families.

Most of the children younger than Bikonzi were naked and being washed by their mothers. While he longed to clean himself as well, Bikonzi found the prospect of nakedness in front of these others–and particularly in front of these guards–far too exposing. He refused to voluntarily undress in the midst of the men who had taken his life from him. He needed to keep something. He rested his weight, leaning back onto his hands, sitting quietly as the sound of quick splashes and trickles bounced off the trees above.

CHAPTER 4:
MANGOES

"A united family eats from the same plate."

-African Proverb

After that first day, things developed a distinct rhythm in the camp. Everyone would typically awaken with the sun as it poured in through the shattered east windows and open door frames, illuminating the room. The air was always filled with dust, tracked into the premises from the bare and battered feet of each family. Bikonzi's first breaths would often be interrupted by coughs as his lungs sought to expel the night from him. Armed guards would be positioned directly outside the warehouse, adjacent to each of the doors. While the doorways were open and accessible, they dared not leave without permission, under the impending silent threat of their guns. On the second day, they were provided one large pot for the whole room. The four families were, in total, given two cups of rice each day and were required to get any water necessary to cook the rice from their trips to the creek. They were also given a chafing dish to heat the pot, and they were intently supervised as they ate. While this process remained civil for the first three or four days, with each family getting a fair section of the rice provided, increased hunger and desperation quickly changed things.

Bikonzi first noticed Traya breaking the trend, as she took considerably more for herself and her children despite having the smallest family in the room. She was a tall woman, strong in will and body, and remained an imposing presence to all who encountered her. On her first attempt at grabbing more rice, she faced verbal resistance from the other mothers, but her cold, dark stare quickly quieted her resisters' objections. By the second attempt, no one even questioned her —she simply took an extra handful as part of the feeding process.

Memories now flooded to B's mind of similar instances in his interactions with Traya—small, moments that moved from unremarkable to noteworthy in his mind given her behavior here and now. A small comment at a gathering between families; a prioritization of her perspective or view at the expense of others; an aggressive response to something not going her way. Perhaps all it takes it a crisis to bring out what has always been true.

The result of her actions had a clear and obvious effect on the rest of the families. They would eagerly wait over the top of the pot as the water heated the rice, ready to grasp as soon as it was finished cooking. On the sixth or seventh day—Bikonzi was noticing that it became difficult to keep track since they had arrived–his youngest brother, Team, reached his hands into the hot water before the rice was finished to grab a few grains and shove it into his mouth quickly— Rose was appalled at this action, immediately pulling Team away from the pot so that she could deliver a prompt spanking. Such punishment did not deter him an ounce: the very next day, he thrust his hands into the boiling water all the same. He was spanked again but continued this over the next few days anyway.

If anyone needed to relieve themselves, they simply did so within the confines of the building. The stench was awful, a rancid and stinging sensory manifestation of the plight of the people within. The guards were always vocal about their annoyance in these instances; should the cries of the mothers and children reach their ears, they would often enter the room abruptly and warn them to keep quiet, using their weapons to point and direct their commands to the entire room. This produced fear and anger in Bikonzi: such seemingly random threats of violence put him persistently on edge.

They continued their trips to the creek, which happened twice in that first week, mainly to reduce the discomfort of their own noses. This allowed the families to stay hydrated as well, and Rose would often soak her garments in the creek so that so that she might squeeze out a few droplets for her children between trips.

It confused Bikonzi as to why they were being given food in the first place. After all, it seemed that their goal was to kill each of these families; why keep prolonging their lives? It moved him, one day just after they had eaten, to ask his mother for an answer.

"Mother, why do they feed us?" he inquired.

"They are confused. They do not know if we are them or they are us," she replied.

"What do you mean 'them' or 'us?'" he asked in return.

"It's a long story, my son…" she replied, patting him on his head as she spoke.

Bikonzi felt his mother pushing his inquiries away with her latest words. His mind jumped again to those soldiers who had come around their home looking for his father. He had always sensed a threatening spirit in their inquiries, and their guns only made that clearer, but he had never really known why. His playground conversations, too, would often be littered with references to these sorts of men or rumors about who they were. Particularly over the last couple of weeks, some of his friends had even spoken of distant violence. "I know a friend of mine whose neighbor's uncle was taken from his family and killed…" was often how they went. Such comments seemed only to confuse him more. Now that such things had broken in to his own experience, though, he felt this was good enough time as any to get some clarity from his mother. He decided to press more on her to help him understand.

"I want to hear the story," he said to his mother after a few silent seconds.

Rose remained silent following his request. She tilted her head slightly upward, her eyes rising in thoughtfulness. After a few moments, she nodded to herself, almost imperceptibly, and turned back toward Bikonzi.

"Alright, I'll tell you the story. A long time ago, long before even your grandparents were born, our land was shared by different clans and tribes. While there were some natural fights between us—even the closest of families have their fights, right?—we all shared a common language, a common culture, and common traditions. We shared well together. But then, right around when your grandmother was born, foreigners came into our land, foreigners with skin like the clouds in the sky."

Bikonzi turned briefly to the broken window pane and glimpsed a small, white cloud, wispy in the sea of light blue that surrounded it. He looked down at his own hand, imagining its color vanishing into a pale, cloudlike hue. He had never seen someone with skin like that - where were they from? Rose continued on before he could ask about them.

"We call these people *muzungu*. And when the *muzungu* arrived, they started lots and lots of new farms in our land: food, rubber—you know, what car tires are made of–wood, gasoline. As they grew these farms, they built whole systems to make them run, and they started to use our tribes and clans to do their work for them. As they did this, they also started to divide us. They split us up over specific traits, talking about how these made us different from one another. They even talked about one tribe–the Tutsis–being better than the other tribe, the Hutus. They divided us over many things: the hue of our skin, our accents, the languages we preferred."

As his mother spoke, Bikonzi's mind ran through the many friends and parents from his school back home. He remembered noticing slightly different shades of skin color or different ways some of his friends' parents spoke. He had never thought much of it—he didn't imagine or see them as any different than he and his family.

"And soon, our clans were officially split from one another. People were given identity cards to show who was who. And soon some of us were treated better than others because of our identity cards. Some of us were given certain jobs, while others were denied those jobs. Some of us were given nicer homes, while others of us weren't. We were told stories about who was better and who was worse. Pretty soon, our whole nation was split up by these categories that the *muzungu* brought in. And people started to get angry at one another over it. Even when many of the *muzungu* left, many of our people still had disagreements and fights over the categories they sorted us into. Eventually, those fights grew bigger and bigger. Governments started to take sides, giving more guns to one side than the other. Wars started—first one, and now a second—over all of this. The men who have been coming to the house see us as worse than them. They've been taught to believe that is true. So, they are sorting us, based upon our language and our accents and our faces."

This made Bikonzi think of the conversation between the two soldiers who had driven them to the camp. When they had pulled the truck over, they had gone back and forth on the way everyone was speaking—the way they sounded.

"Is that why they didn't kill us on the road? They were confused about who we were?"

"Yes. They heard us speaking their language, and they were confused. They are feeding us now because we sound like we are them."

Bikonzi paused.

"Are we them?"

Rose smiled slightly, touching Bikonzi's cheek and looking him in the eyes.

"Yes, and no. We are human. We are not bullies."

Their conversation ended there, with Bikonzi's mind swirling over the details. He couldn't get the story out of his head that night as he tried to fall asleep. While the soldiers might have felt 'confused,' he was not. Whether or not they spoke the same language, whether or not they had families–he recalled the photograph he had seen hanging from the belt of the guard before–He hated these men for taking away his life, for preventing him from having the things he had before, for paralyzing him in anger and inaction.

He became fixated on the soldiers that night. He intuited that they must live on or near the camp, as he could often hear voices not far off from their warehouse and sometimes could even make out music from radio signals. He wondered what their lives were like. They were only a few hundred feet away, yet their experience must be so different. They had enough food to spare—at least considerably more than what was given in the pot each day—and clean water to drink. They had clothes that weren't tattered and torn and hats or sunglasses to protect them from the sun. How could they not see what they were doing? It amazed him what a few feet could change. He fell asleep that night with such thoughts ruling his mind.

It did not take long for the food to stop. Bikonzi figured the soldiers must have become less confused about the identity of the prisoners, or they had simply received confirmed orders from the commanders to initiate the removal of food. They took the pot from the room, and rice deliveries ceased. He figured that the guards must be appreciative of this, as they would no longer need to enter the room as often to support the families. He felt sure that they despised seeing and smelling the residents.

Though each family had only received a cup of rice a day, the elimination of it altogether made noticeable differences in the families. B saw this, particularly within his siblings. After two of these foodless days, Amiee, John, and Moses all seemed to shrink, their clothes hanging off of their bodies more loosely than before. Seth and Team became bloated, their bellies extending out beyond shriveling legs. Everyone became lethargic, often spending their hours lying down, only moving when it was absolutely necessary. They were all dying, even faster than they had been before.

Two nights after the food had stopped, Bikonzi was preparing to sleep. His stomach pains prolonged the process; he fought to find the least uncomfortable position possible. In this process, he overheard a conversation between his two older brothers.

"We can't keep going like this," John said, speaking to Moses. He hushed his voice enough to avoid detection from Amiee or Rose, one of whom was asleep and the other of whom was tending to Team, who cried on this night. Bikonzi shifted his focus to the conversation of his brothers, both out of curiosity and a desire to cease thinking about his own hunger. He eavesdropped on their conversation from a few feet away as he rolled over to them to hear better. In the darkness, he felt he could avoid detection well enough. Sparse moonlight shone into the room in spurts.

"We need food. Team is already getting weak. His legs look like twigs," he continued.

"Well, yes. But how are we going to get it? We can't even get out of this building. The guards are constantly making rounds and stationed outside. Besides, they only live a few yards away," Moses replied, answering Bikonzi's suspicions about the residence of the soldiers.

John paused, took a deep breath, and glanced around. B thought John might have seen him spying on their conversation, but if he had, he would not have taken any action to correct him.

"I know," John said, "But we're next to the road where we came into the camp that first day. I woke up yesterday to the sound of people shuffling and talking together just before the sun rose. When I woke up again today, the same thing happened. People walk by every morning."

Moses seemed confused as to what this meant or why it was helpful, and Bikonzi echoed the same confusion in his head.

"I think they are the wives and families of the soldiers. I don't know where they go—probably for water at a well or somewhere for work. They are always in a large group. I think, if I time it right, I can sneak out without the guards noticing. Then I can just walk along the road with everyone else."

"What? No way. You won't even get through the door," Moses scoffed.

Bikonzi hated John's idea, too. He couldn't imagine his oldest brother disappearing into the night in the same way his father had. His stomach grumbled as he tossed these thoughts over—John and Moses continued.

"The guards change their shift at the same time every day, just before the sun rises, and most nights, the guards outside this doorway are sleeping when the change is made. I think it could be dark enough to slip by them—then I could hide out of the side until the crowd comes along and join them without anyone noticing." John reasoned.

Moses was stunned, eyes wide and staring back incredulously. "How will you get back in? The guards are here all day."

"I'll do the same thing. If all of these people leave each day, that means they come back each day. There's only one road in and out of the camp."

"What if they notice you? You'll be walking right next to them. How do you know they won't turn you in?" he replied.

"I don't."

The two words hung in the air, floating above them all. Bikonzi's mind pictured what John's attempts might look like, and all he could see was failure. The sound and sight of the butt of a gun into his back kept returning to his mind to him after Daniel's episode; in those few seconds, all he could picture was John's agonizing face.

Moses was silent now. He stared at John, whose eyes remained locked to his. It seemed to Bikonzi as if they were internally working, somehow together, to see if there was any other way.

"We need food," John repeated, "There are mango trees just beyond the initial tree line; I saw them on our last walk to the creek."

Moses looked down now, raising his hand to his face and resting his cheek in it.

"You know they'll punish you if you get caught. They might kill you."

John paused, looking down as well.

"I know. But they are already killing me now. They are killing us all."

They were silent for a long time. John raised his hand and wrapped it around the back of Moses's neck, bringing their heads together.

Bikonzi quietly slid out of sight and propped himself against the cold concrete wall, a shiver coursing through him as he did. He began to survey his family, putting together their current states using the scattered streaks of moonlight. Rose quieted Team, whose cry had dulled to a groan as he tried to sleep. Amiee held Seth, both of them sleeping as best they could. Jay rested her head just next to B, her hands pinned under her face. And now, after listening to his elder brothers discuss how they could provide for the family, he began to consider his own role. Their present state had created a seeming dividing line between young and old, vulnerable and capable, a line which ran directly through him. Bikonzi was utterly conflicted: in one sense, he was the oldest of the younger siblings and certainly could group himself with them as their time in the camp progressed, needing regular care and attention.

But he felt a pull away from that sort of vulnerability. He did not want his own health to be the concern of his older siblings and mother. He wanted to be self-sufficient, providing for his own health; he did not want to force Rose, Amiee, John, and Moses to care for him in the same way they were required to for the youngest children. The more he thought, the more he agreed with John: Death had arrived, and so it was not something to fear as before. It was no longer a feeling in his mind but an embodied reality around him. He was inside of him and inside of his family; He churned his stomach and decayed his body. His constancy was like a wall enclosing them all. *I'm going to die if I stay in this room anyway*, he thought, *and when I do, I will be less of a burden to the rest of my family. I might as well try to do something with the life I have left.* It was time for him to respond. He did not yet know how or whether it would even be possible, but he had decided at this point. From here forward, his mind would be fixed on self-sufficient resistance by any means necessary.

As the night wore on, Bikonzi fought off sleep as best he could. He wanted to be sure he was awake to see if John would sneak out at dawn. He attempted to keep an eye open at all times, which proved nearly impossible. His eyes, already sufficiently dry from the lack of water in his system, became uncomfortably so almost immediately. Resistance was more challenging with each passing hour. He thus resorted to closing his eyes but focusing his listening capacity on any sound he heard. He dozed off a few times, but given the preoccupation of his mind, rarely found himself sliding off into deeper dreams, and at any realization of the waking of others, he snapped his eyes open quickly. This process continued for hours and was a painful one for B. Sleep was the one area in which escape from hunger, thirst, and pain was at least somewhat possible, and resisting that relief proved trying. Yet he persisted, and as the light began to turn a deep blue through the windows, he heard someone stir.

Bikonzi casually rolled himself onto his other side in the direction of the noise, briefly opening his right eye as he did so. He noticed, blurry though his vision was at the early hour, John began to pull himself up into a squatting position. Moses lay just to his right, and John gently shook him awake. Moses's eyes opened, and he rubbed them as he began to sit up. B knew he was not likely to be noticed by his brothers with the lack of clear light, but he nevertheless slowed and focused his breathing to remain as silent as possible.

He now heard John and Moses begin to whisper calmly and steadily. Some children stirred in their sleep around the room, harmonizing with the sound of distant crickets, creating a soft sheet of noise to cover their conversation. John remained balanced on his toes as if ready to jump at any moment. Moses looked to be stating a case as he sat before him, his hands pleading but his words muffled. After a few more comments back and forth, John pushed Moses's hands away, and the boys were silent for a few brief seconds. Then John began to move to the nearest door, Moses watching intently.

Bikonzi sat up quietly, straining his neck and squinting his eyes to catch the shadows amidst the bluish darkness. John remained squatted as he moved, his steps somehow silent on the broken concrete floor. Upon arrival at the doorway, he simply stopped. The outline of his head turned so that his right ear faced out into the morning. He sat like this, with a hand grasped tightly on the inside of the wall, for minutes. Bikonzi caught himself holding his breath in silence, every sense heightened. He noticed the steady pump of his heart, the chill of his toes, the sweat beginning to moisten his palms. He gulped dryly as he watched. Voices began to arise outside, speaking lightly to one another as footsteps pattered upon the dirt. He glimpsed Moses, who sat unmoving just feet away, still unaware of B. He seemed to be mimicking John's posture, squatting himself as he watched his brother. Then suddenly, without warning or noise, John's silhouette slipped through the doorway. Bikonzi sat and stared for a few more seconds, blinking as if expecting John to reappear suddenly, but he did not. There was only silence. As Moses began to turn back to the family, B swiftly rolled over to avoid detection. He ensured his back was to Moses, implying sleep, yet he remained wide awake, his eyes rerunning the vision of John's disappearance.

The sun shone into the room only an hour later, and Bikonzi had not been able to sleep since John had left. As the rest of his family began waking, he stirred to make it appear as if he had been asleep the entire night as well.

It did not take long for everyone to realize John was missing. Amiee was the first to notice, immediately concerned, asking her mother if she knew what had happened. Rose said nothing in response. She scanned the entire room to ensure John was not present, and then she directed her attention toward Moses, who was beginning to wake. She did not say a word to him, only stared, and Moses sat silently before her, eyes peering into hers. Amiee watched this interaction with immense confusion.

"Where is he?!" Amiee asked again, adjusting Seth in her arms. She was frustrated with the lack of speech from both Rose and Moses.

"I don't know, but he will be back," Rose responded as she tended to her other waking children. Bikonzi noticed an unwaveringness in her voice. Faith emanated from her. This was not to say she was without weakness or frailty; indeed, she had already shown signs of fatigue, losing muscle in her arms and legs. She rarely smiled. Yet something in her maintained a sense of confidence amidst her pain. It didn't make sense to Bikonzi: she clearly was suffering and did not overlook it, and yet she continued in steady endurance, never flinching in front of her family. He wondered if this was a sense of faith in God that kept her this way. As long as he could remember, his mother was deeply religious; indeed, their entire family was. Bikonzi's father had played music at their church growing up, and his grandfather preached sermons regularly. There was a charisma to those services that Bikonzi didn't quite grasp. People would dance and shout, sing and clap, smile and cry every week, and he would watch.

Yet now there was no dancing. Singing and smiling were utterly absent. He wondered how this faith could persist when the surroundings had changed so clearly. *What is faith when God is gone?* He asked himself. He was entirely sure there was no answer. No God that could give the joy he witnessed in church as a child could also give the pain he saw now to the same people. He considered his mother's enduring faith unhelpful. Perhaps it could mentally ease the immensity of the pain they were relegated to, but it could do nothing to change things. It was only neglecting the inevitable in this camp.

As he worked through these questions in his own mind, Rose gathered her children together and prayed. 'What God would still be listening?' he thought to himself as he closed his eyes and bowed his head.

That day dragged on from there. Bikonzi waited eagerly, still keeping the secret from Moses that he knew John had gone to obtain food for the family. He was certainly concerned for his brother but also desirous: he was quite hungry, and the notion of food, regardless of the type, left him quite excited.

The sun began to set again, the sky returning to the deep blue it had been when John had left that morning. Bikonzi noticed an anxiousness in Moses; he fidgeted his fingers, tapping against his knees as he sat hunched next to the door. It didn't seem that Moses had noticed, but B also saw Rose keenly keeping Moses in her sight that night, watching him as he waited. It was as if she knew what had happened.

Suddenly, Bikonzi noted voices a long way off. He had heard them before each day but had never taken much notice; now, it was the only thing he heard. Their steps became louder. B could hear them through the numerous open doorways as they passed. He could make out a few specific words, conversations about work, food, and the weather. And then, the voices passed. They faded out into the distance, into the night, as quickly as they had entered. John had not yet returned to the room. B noticed Moses sink his head into his bundled body. The only sound now was crickets.

Minutes passed by in this silence. Moses did not move or raise his head, and it looked as if Rose was holding back tears as she watched her son. Bikonzi began to consider what could have happened. Had he gotten lost? Was he found and killed? Did he run away? Many thoughts filled his head without an answer.

The night had gotten dark, and visibility was becoming low again. Bikonzi moved toward Moses to console him, but suddenly, a quiet whisper—as if from a ghost—sounded through the doorway.

"I have mangoes," the voice quietly said.

Moses looked up instantaneously, eyes full of hope at the voice he recognized. Bikonzi turned toward it, and Rose sat up in curiosity. John had come back into the room.

He somehow held two mangoes in each hand; they looked largely green and under-ripe from what he could see. Rose jumped to embrace John tenderly, joined by Moses and Amiee. Bikonzi also wrapped his arms around his siblings and mother. Rose began to cry softly.

"Quiet," John said softly. "We need to make sure they don't know that I ever left. Quick, let's eat."

Rose nodded, acknowledging John's sentiment. She grabbed a broken piece of chipped concrete from the jagged floor and began to break into the fruit, sectioning off chunks for each child. John assisted in this, rushing his actions as he did; it was clear he was still worried about the possibility of the guards entering and discovering the food. After cutting them into pieces, John and Rose began to distribute them amongst the family, from youngest to oldest. Bikonzi was surprised by this initially: whenever they ate at home, his parents and oldest siblings would eat first, and youngest siblings thereafter. The more dire need of the youngest siblings now, however, changed the order of things. After taking care of Team,

Seth, and Jay, John provided a chunk to B's opened hand, the light green fruit dripping a bit from the crude cutting. Without hesitation, he shoved it into his mouth.

Upon the first bite, a sour taste exploded into the many empty cracks and spaces. Immediately, his jaw tightened, and his eyes squinted, adjusting to the rush of new flavor. His mouth began to water in response. The mango was crunchy, vegetable-like in its texture, engaging B's teeth for the first time in days. He continued to chew through it, adjusting to the sourness, and a pleasant sigh involuntarily emerged from him. No fruit had ever tasted as delicious as this one; no food had meant so much to him. He examined his family as they ate: they were smiling and sharing affectionate gazes with one another, relishing together in the experience of a new taste and color. John continued handing out more fruit pieces to them, prompting multiple servings for each. *Maybe this is where God is.* B thought to himself, taking his final bite. He savored it again, allowing the taste to fill him.

CHAPTER 5:
DEATH

"Don't think there are no crocodiles
just because the water is calm."
-African Proverb

Mangoes became the fruit of life. After this initial successful journey, John developed a rhythm. He would travel every other day, gathering as much as he could into his hands and his shirt. This often meant three or four mangoes for the entire family, and they were promptly devoured upon delivery. Given the time of year, they were not often the vibrant yellow-orange Bikonzi had remembered mangoes to be at home. Instead, the peel had a speckled green tint, was firm, and was almost resistant to being cut open. Their flesh was a pale yellow, crispy, and tart, yet it didn't matter to anyone. Any amount of food was a gift.

It did not take long for the other boys in the room to recognize his success and join him for these excursions; after all, not much remained hidden in a room this large. After two of John's mango trips, a collective of six would rotate through in shifts. They would often go together, though usually no more than two at a time, sneaking past the guards just before dusk out the single doorway in the same manner John did. They all found this provided adequate support while still avoiding detection. The need for survival had developed an efficient system.

The guards had also become significantly less stringent in their watch. Those who took the night shift often slept through it, which allowed ample time and space for the boys to continue their work.

Though they succeeded in each successive trip, and even with the reduced attentiveness of the guards, this did not ease Rose's concern. The trips seemed to her like the taste of the mangoes: sour but necessary. B watched her each of the days that either of her sons had left and saw this clearly. She would regularly glance at the door for their re-entry, even in the middle of the day, and she would promptly turn her head at the slightest noise from outside the room. Yet each time, without fail, they would return with life in their hands and clothes.

It stung Bikonzi to be left in the room each time, watching his older brothers risk their lives for the sake of him and his family. He felt burdensome, a dead weight being carried like the youngest children in the place. He knew he wanted to provide for himself, to prevent his family from needing to care for him, and he waited eagerly for the opportunity to present itself.

One evening, a pitiful moaning came from the other side of the room. It was utterly unfamiliar to him, like the call of a strange and foreign animal. It started low, from the gut, and ended in the throat, scratchy and dry, as if moving up the body. He glanced over at the noise, alongside each of the other boys in front of him, curious and captivated. At first, he could not tell who was making the noise: there was a crowd of small children and infants, and amidst the sparse light at dusk, it took another two groans for him to pinpoint the source. Finally, his eyes aligned with his ears, finding a woman's body collapsed in the corner of the room. The abysmal sounds were coming from David and Christian's mother, Eden.

While difficult to see, B noticed that she was scrunched in pain, a grimace unmoving across her face. She was clutching tightly to Abel, who was still wrapped in the same bed sheets as the night they were captured. She rocked herself back and forth in the fetal position, maintaining a steady and dull groaning, which remained a baseline for her more painful outbursts. Both of her eldest sons moved quickly from the crowd of boys around John and gathered tightly around their mother. David promptly grabbed the baby while Christian tended to her, asking what was going on and what she needed. She did not answer, only continuing her rocking and moaning accordingly. Rose joined the sons, holding and sitting next to her; they had been good friends for years, raising boys of similar ages, and her compassion was visible in her posture.

That entire night was soundtracked by her struggling. While there were fluctuations in volume and intensity as she fell in and out of sleep, the noises were steady, often waking Bikonzi, startled and afraid. He attempted to turn his back to the noises, which helped with the level of sound, though only slightly. At one point, he thought he heard the sound of vomit from her, spilling softly upon the floor. He had no idea what had happened to her, what had caused this sudden outburst of pain and suffering, and he wondered if the same might happen to him. Or if the same might happen to his own mother.

The next morning brought sunlight, but did not bring with it healing. Instead, somehow, her pain intensified. Whether due to lack of sleep or an escalating condition, her moans and cries rang out louder than before. Rose still sat beside her, now rubbing her back as she attempted to comfort her. The sunlight revealed beads of sweat that had gathered on her face and soaked into her clothes, which now clung tightly to her body. She managed to muster up strength enough to utter broken sentences. B was only able to hear a few words in the midst of her pain. She spoke of her stomach hurting and mentioned her baby and mangoes multiple times. Rose nodded in response and began to sing softly.

"Olele, Olele! Moliba makasi."

B remembered the words from his childhood; it was a lullaby his mother would sing to him as he lay in bed.

"Mboka na ye! Mboka na ye! Mboka mboka Kasaii."

She seemed to quiet a bit as she listened, her cries becoming more scattered.

"Eh, eho! Benguela aya. Eh, eho!"

The rhythm of the tune seemed to have a powerful effect on her. Her body eased its fluctuations, her breaths became deeper and less frequent, and her grimace began to fade slightly.

Bikonzi noticed a strange peace fall over him as he listened and watched. His heart was warmed, enveloped by a lyrical blanket, securing him and slowing him. He raised his hand to his chest, feeling a slowing, steady beat. And for that brief moment, the day slipped away. He was returned to his own home, returned to the safety of his bed, returned to the freedom of careless lyrics and melodies. It was as if he had escaped.

It was then that two of the guards entered the place, their angry calls drowning out the peaceful words from Rose.

"What is going on in here?!" the first of them yelled, eyes wide and scanning the room.

"She is sick," Rose answered. She was prompt and direct, refraining from elevating her voice.

They looked quickly down at Eden, who remained quiet. Her head rested on the concrete floor, turning to them with weak eyes and a stoic gaze. Then, as a surprise to all in the room, she spoke, her voice muffled and dry.

"Please," she pleaded. "My baby... I can't feed…"

She coughed and turned before continuing.

"He needs... hospital. Help..."

It seemed she had poured her entire energy into those short, broken phrases. The guards' expressions hardly changed. They glanced first at the child, then back at Eden, and finally at one another. They whispered briefly. Bikonzi could not make out their words.

Suddenly, as abruptly as they had entered the room, they moved forth and grabbed Eden, each of them by one arm. Christian and David jumped forward in response but were promptly cast aside. They dragged her outside, and her screams were worse than the night before. She yelled, her voice cutting with every word.

"My baby! You need to help him! My baby!"

Once they had left the room, B ran swiftly to the broken windows of the place to watch them. Others followed, at the resistance of their mothers, and climbed onto and around one another to try to peek through the window.

The first of the guards threw her over his shoulder, carrying her off while the other held a gun to her. Her words grew less distinct and loud as they moved farther away as if she had resigned to their grasp. After they had disappeared out of sight and into one of the military buildings on the premises, the children gathered around the window and returned to their parents. Rose moved back to her family, bringing them all close together and wrapping her arms around each of them. That was the last Bikonzi ever saw of Eden. Christian's hopeful comments about the angel rang in the back of Bikonzi's head, and he was sad he had ever been mad at him. He hoped now more than ever that he was right. He couldn't imagine losing his own mother.

It did not take long for Abel to expire next. The guards never returned for the child, and he was too small to eat mangoes. By the time they came three days later for a trip to the creek for water, he had ceased breathing. Upon arrival to the room, the same guards who had taken Eden away noticed the baby. Seeing his condition, the soldier motioned with a head nod to his accompanying guard, silently urging him to take the rest of the room to the creek. As they were shuffled out the doorway, B looked back and saw the guard standing over the child, holding his gun loosely in his right hand as he simply stared down at the lifeless body. By the time they returned to the room, the baby was gone.

Death had now taken up residence in their midst, making himself comfortable. No longer was he moving across the camp at large or acting as a potential or hypothetical presence. Now, he had intimately infiltrated the rancid room. It would have been enough had he stopped there, simply a presence already known but closer in proximity. But he was not content with remaining an external force. He pressed in until he had wormed his way into Bikonzi's dreams. Image after image ruled the night. Of Eden rolling in pain. Of her wailing over the shoulder of the guard. Of the stillness of Abel. The moments regularly replayed, dominating his subconscious for days.

It was hard for Bikonzi to know whether sleeping or lying awake was worse. When he slept, he gained bits of rest but often awoke in the midst of painful reminders, sweating and breathing heavily. When he lay awake, he stared into nothingness; he could replace the images with utter blackness, devoid of sentiment and increasingly exhausted. Sleep was thus intermittent for him.

With this lack of sleep came an increased awareness of the goings on in the room at nighttime. During the awakened portions of his midnight bouts, B noticed a trend in his mother. She would often rise from sleep, glancing around at her children as she sat up. B would squint his eyes to appear asleep, all the while maintaining his gaze upon her shadowed figure in the night. Once sure that she had not woken anyone, she would promptly stand and move outside the room. Though he did not know where she went, B knew she was not venturing far, for he could hear faint noises from outside: coughs and grunts, heaves and moans. Then, after a brief silence, she would return, assume her place next to her children, and fall back to sleep. He did not know how she managed to slip past the guards and avoid them on these evenings. Perhaps they simply watched her as she did this.

These moments of listening reminded him of Eden. Her sickness, whatever it had been, had produced similar reactions and noises. The noises themselves only furthered his dread, accompanying the visual reminders in the night as he turned, questions burning in his brain.

For as much effort and care as she took to keep these trips hidden from her children, Rose was eventually unable to keep her secret. One morning, not long after Bikonzi had first noticed her nighttime trips out of the room, she was struck by some sort of physical ailment, quickly running to the corner of the room and vomiting. It was just before David and Moses had left the room for more mangoes, and they abruptly turned, along with the rest of the room, when they heard Rose vomiting. She leaned herself against the wall, supporting her weight with her right arm while holding her clothes tightly against her chest.

John and Amiee rushed to her, showing immediate concern and shock. Moses joined them, and B attempted to match their surprise. He had known that she was not feeling well, but he did not know who else might have an indication. As he moved closer to Rose and his siblings, he scanned the other families to see their reactions. Every person with age enough to understand looked on with quiet curiosity; having just seen what happened only a few days before, there was a natural concern. Bikonzi also noticed that Traya looked on with intensity, eyes focused, and lips pursed, watching like a lion crouched in tall grass.

Rose continued to vomit for multiple minutes as they all silently watched on, her body contracting with each wave. After it had passed, she stood quietly, unmoving, a gasp escaping from her mouth. Following a few frozen moments, Amiee blurted the obvious question:

"What's wrong?"

Rose did not respond immediately. Her breathing had started to slow. They all hung on her response.

"I have been feeling this for a while. I've tried to ignore it," she finally responded.

She turned as she said these words, stepped toward her family, and crouched. She smiled and looked up into their eyes, pausing for a few brief seconds with each of them. She stroked B's face as she arrived at him. Her hand was warm and soft, moistened by sweat. Then, with each of them waiting, confused and overwhelmed, she spoke again.

"I'm pregnant."

The family was frozen. B angled his head slightly, widening his eyes in a mixture of confusion and shock. He glanced quickly at his siblings: John and Amiee were unphased as if they had already known. Moses matched B's expression. Jay immediately smiled, flashing white teeth not seen in weeks. The youngest children sat aimlessly nearby, unable to understand the nature of the revelation. No one spoke.

"I felt it start just after the first day in the jail. My head started to hurt. Nausea. I was tired. I thought it might be all of this, but I'm sure now. I'm pregnant." Rose elaborated.

B noticed genuine anger in her voice, maybe for the first time in weeks.

"It doesn't seem right. It shouldn't happen this way. It shouldn't..."

Rose trailed off, looking down to avoid showing her tears. Amiee slowly moved toward her, tears in her eyes, and wrapped her arms around her. Moses and Jay mimicked this action, and Bikonzi followed suit, picking up Team as he did. John stood behind her, placing his hand on her back.

"I love you all."

The words trembled from her lips, fear and ambiguity moving with them. B could not recall a time he had seen her more shaken. His mind flashed again to Eden and Abel; they still lived in his brain. He blinked hard and lightly shook his head as if they might fly out his ear. He then glimpsed Seth and Team. He saw their thin, wiry legs. He saw their bloated bellies. He saw their eyes, red and locked onto their mother.

Following her revelation, it became obvious to everyone else that she was pregnant. Soon, her skirt began to rip at the seams, threatening to come undone altogether. The next evening, John and Christian returned from their latest mango trip with new clothes for Rose to replace the dirtied and ripped set she wore. John had claimed that they could make their way to the market and swipe the clothes undetected. Upon being handed these, B noted a glisten in Rose's eyes as she looked upon John, a half-smile even creeping upon her face.

At this point, Bikonzi was first struck with a realization about these trips out of the camp. On each journey, the boys had every chance to simply run away and never return. Yet they didn't. He wondered why, when freedom was upon them, they chose to return. Then he recalled that first night, hiding under the bed, with his own chance to flee. And he remembered that overwhelming urge to call out to his mother, to be held in her presence, to be with his family. As it turns out, he knew–in some unutterable way–exactly why they returned.

CHAPTER 6:

LIFE

"If the full moon loves you, why worry about the stars?"

-African Proverb

A curious trend had begun at the camp following the loss of Eden and Rose's revelation. It only took a couple of days for Bikonzi to notice: the guards were relaxing their watch over the room. It may have been a matter of manpower, as trucks were coming and going along the road regularly, taking soldiers along with them; perhaps there were soldiers needed elsewhere. Regardless, they had reduced their presence immediately outside the doors of the room to just two guards overnight, and the only other time they entered the room was for trips to the creek. On the latest of these walks, the Moise boys heard news that perked their ears.

Two guards arrived early in the morning to relieve the night shift, and the new arrivals shuffled each of the families out toward the creek again, both of them remaining at the back of the crowd this time. The Moises were thrust out last, and thus John, Moses, and Bikonzi remained within earshot of guards' whispering.

"We still don't know," the first guard began.

"Yes, we do. We know these people. We took them from their homes," the second replied.

"Then why do they speak Lingala?"

A pause occurred before the next response, and the first continued.

"Since we can't know for sure, I just say we use them while we have them."

"What do you mean?"

"I mean, use them for work. There's so much we need done…"

By this time, John and Moses had already made eye contact with one another and, without speaking, shared a thousand words. It was clear they were considering ideas on what 'use them' might mean and how they might benefit from becoming beneficial to the soldiers. B noticed their nonverbal excitement and echoed it less subtly. A cunning smile came across his face as he turned to John and Moses. His obviousness alerted one of the guards. A foot landed into Bikonzi's back first and then into Moses's and John's in succession.

"Keep walking!"

John glared at Bikonzi as they continued moving forward; he had single-handedly ended the conversation before it proceeded into any detail and ultimately kept all of them without an idea of what might be meant by the comments. Bikonzi forced his head down and continued to walk in silence.

Later that night, as the moon shone in through the empty window frames, brighter than B had remembered, the same two guards who had escorted the families to the creek that morning now sat watch. They were both seated next to the doorway on the north side of the building. Laying close to the wall, John, Moses, and Bikonzi all strained to hear their conversation again.

"You really think they would get away?" one laughed at the other.

"No fence... what stops them?" the other responded.

"Fear. What's worse, this place or the open jungle? Besides, most of them are children. They aren't bold enough to begin with."

"True... I am sick of sitting here every night."

"Exactly. Why not use them."

"Why not kill them?"

"Well, yes, eventually. But we might as well get something out of them first. Besides, think about it: they may just die while they work. Did you see them this morning? Skin and bones."

"What about Commander Andre? He's not easy."

"He doesn't have to know. Even if we tell him, he'd take free labor. Besides, the last thing he wants is blood on his hands and then to find out he got it wrong. Using them would postpone a decision and help all of us out."

They sat in silence a bit longer. Crickets filled the void.

The men continued on, trailing into other conversations, but the three boys had heard all they needed. Bikonzi laid back down; his imagination flooded with ideas about the new potential at the camp.

John first offered to work for the guards. The next morning, after eavesdropping on these latest two conversations, he gained the attention of one of them as they stepped away from their building, concluding their night shift.

"I'll work for you," he said plainly, standing in the doorway.

Both men turned back at him. They smiled and chuckled lightly, looking him up and down. The other boys moved closer to John, remaining out of sight of the doorway but inches away from him. It was silent for a few seconds before one of the guards spoke.

"What do you know how to do, cockroach?" he asked.

"I can do anything you need me to," John responded unflinchingly.

Again, silence.

The guards whispered, indiscernible to those in the room, and then spoke.

"Boy, come with us."

John stepped slowly out of the doorway, looked back briefly into the room, and then continued forward. Rose held back tears but did not speak. B watched as John walked alongside them. One guard grabbed his arm and shoved him forward, and both men held guns as encouragement to keep walking. They continued along the road and eventually fell out of sight.

Just as it had been on that first day, John had gone to get mangoes, but this day dragged. Bikonzi could not keep his mind from running through potential scenarios: what if John returned bruised? What if he came back with food he had stolen? What if he never came back at all? The last thought scared him the most; he wasn't sure what their family would do without John. It was clear that Rose didn't know either. While she was attempting to mask her emotions when he was taken, it was clear to Bikonzi that his absence shook her. All they could do was wait.

The sun began to set that evening, and as the yellow of the day meshed with the purple of dusk, John appeared in the doorway. He was sweaty, covered in dirt and grime, and smirking only slightly. Upon walking in, he was embraced immediately by Rose, whose tears now flowed freely. Their family crowded around him, surrounded by a few of the other boys. Traya's family remained in their corner of the room, farther from windows where light could penetrate. In the midst of their excitement, the Moises didn't realize that John was holding a bag. He carried a burlap sack full of something. Everyone stepped back briefly and did not speak, simply waiting on John's explanation of the item he held.

He widened his eyes, expanding his smile as he did. Looking around at the fellow family members and boys, he reached into the bag and pulled out an overflowing handful of white rice. As if already coordinated, each family member's eyes rose excitedly in unison. They crowded closely around him, moths to a flame. Steam still evaporated from the handful. B drew his face close and could feel the warmth ever so slightly drawn toward his face. It was not much, but it was something other than mangoes.

"At the end of the day, I was helping sweep inside one of the houses for a woman. I think she is married to one of the guards. Just as I was wrapping up, she came over to me and quickly gave me some rice," John began to explain, realizing he had the entire room's attention.

"She said, 'Here, take this. Don't tell anyone I gave this to you.' So I thanked her, grabbed the bag, and left as quickly as I could."

A few scattered smiles responded in the crowd. John chose to split the rice fairly amongst everyone, resulting in about two handfuls for each family.

Bikonzi wasted little time consuming the few grains he had obtained, and though he wished there was more, he did not regret the immediate shoving of the food into his mouth. It was soft and warm as he ate. He did not notice much flavor, but the texture remained distinct as he chewed. Starchy and soft, it was easily broken up and devoured in seconds. It would not fill his stomach, but it had started to fill his spirit. As he swallowed the cooked grains, he was overwhelmed by a feeling he remembered faintly, as if from a dream. It was like something inside of him had been lit. A switch had been turned on and flooded the cavernous reaches of his being. He felt his heart beat a little faster; his toes started to move involuntarily in anticipation. No words came to mind to describe this, no frame for such a shift, yet he somehow felt something was changing. He did not know what it would look like, nor whether his positive feeling was accurate or helpful, but he was sure of one thing: he would leave that room.

John's prosperous return emboldened each of the boys. Only a few days later, Moses, Fistan, David, Christian, and Gideon, another of the boys, Traya's son, joined. Even Daniel, who still remained hobbled from the abuse he suffered those first nights, joined in, leaving the room to work in various ways in the camp. As they each left, Bikonzi intentionally remained, resisting his urge to join the other boys. He knew that if he approached to work for the guards alongside the older boys, he would be immediately discredited due to his size. He had to be more strategic in his approach.

Once he had confirmed they were all out of earshot, B waited a few more minutes before starting forward. He stepped out of the room, walking through the door frame on the west side.

It was cool as he stepped, shaded from the sun. He moved efficiently but quietly, attempting to avoid as much noise as possible. For the first time since their arrival, he was glad to be barefoot, as each pace made less noise on the dry and rocky ground. His eyes remained up and forward, scanning to ensure none of the other boys could see or hear him approaching. He heard Amiee from inside the room whispering urgently.

"Get back here!" she angrily voiced, her teeth clenched together in urgency.

Bikonzi ignored her words and continued toward the edge of the warehouse to attain a view of the rest of the camp. Upon reaching the northwestern corner, he took in the entire space; this was the most comprehensive angle he had obtained since their arrival.

The first thing he noticed, made obvious by its closeness to the room, was the road: it curled its way across the entire camp like a massive snake. Scattered trees lined the side, providing sporadic shade from the intense sun. Turning right, he could see that the road led into a thick jungle, barely cleared away enough for a car to drive under the canopy. He could not see far in that direction as the road disappeared into darkness. He concluded that this must have been how they had been driven into the place and where the military trucks were regularly coming and going. Following the road, his head scanned left. A few steps away, across the road from him directly, were four crudely constructed holes; he remembered the day they had arrived, watching as his brothers dug. He remembered what he had felt in the dirt and quickly moved his eyes further along the road.

From this, it curved sharply to the right and continued toward the horizon. As it did, he noticed many buildings placed on either side. The first was a long, thin structure surrounded by a variety of military weapons and vehicles, and it was placed to the left of the road just along the first curve. He presumed this was where the guards lived. Continuing his scan further, he noticed three more houses along the roadside, each with what appeared—as clear as B could tell—to be gardens or plants. Two were placed on the right and one on the left of the road as it began to curve again, this time to the left in the distance. Finally, the road concluded a few more feet after this second curve, a rounded end buffered by houses on both the near side and far side. He remembered John's description of the soldier's wives, and B assumed they must live in some of these houses. He continued forward slowly, keeping his eyes out for any of his peers.

Bikonzi felt at once freed and terrified in his first venture outside the confines of the room. In the case of the former, B felt incredible relief, as if something had been lifted from his shoulders. Though he had made trips to the creek before, he had always felt under constant threat, but on this occasion, eyes were not bearing down on him as he moved from the cold, dark, broken concrete to the warm, bright, open space of the camp. He was moving because he had chosen to move.

He was also reminded of what this choice could mean for his family. He pictured the faces he had left in the room from the shallow hole. Rose and Amiee immediately filled his mind. This moved him to turn back briefly toward the room, which now sat dozens of feet behind him. Looking over his shoulder, he had to squint as his eyes adjusted to the light around him, and peering into the north doorway, he began to see. He could initially only perceive outlines and eyes in the dark, huddled close together, a purplish hue engulfing them. The light shone strongly upon the side of the building and onto the dry dirt of the adjacent road, reflecting off every surface it touched. Yet it did not penetrate the room. He was abruptly reminded that his movement beyond those walls meant a movement away from familiar safety. He also remembered the presence of Death in that place, and he knew that this safety was a lie. There was no safety. Given his closeness, then, there was no risk. The worst Death could do would be to relieve him.

He considered his next steps, noticing a house about eighty feet to the northwest of him and sitting adjacent to the road. He directed his course there, tiptoeing toward the north wall to again have cover to stand and think. He first moved to pin his back against the building; the outer walls were dark, and he felt this would be a more effective way to remain unseen from his current position rather than being exposed to the open land and sunlight. He slid his body northward along the side of the wall until he could turn the corner. He realized he had been taking shallow, if any, breaths and was filled with nervousness. He did not know what was ahead of him. As much as he had dreamed of getting out of the room, he had not yet truly finalized what to do when he made it. So, he began to consider his potential options.

The first thing that came to mind was his body: since he was not as old or as physically strong as any of the other boys who had set out, he was at a disadvantage. He could not lift or work in the same way. He looked down at himself. His tank top revealed thin and long arms, and the lack of food over the last few weeks had shrunken them down to appear nearly absent of muscle altogether. His legs were similar: thin and wiry, without much substance or support. He felt small and miserable.

And that was when he realized. He did not need strength or even ability; each of the other boys was comparable in their own strength, aside from Daniel, and therefore, none of them were noteworthy in this regard. But B was the youngest and most vulnerable. He was smaller and feebler than the rest of the boys. So, he knew he would need to use those strengths to his benefit; he would use his vulnerability as his strength. He did not yet know how, but he knew that this was his best chance. He would earn the rewards of work without working at all or working very little; he would win with sympathy. With this set in his mind, he strove forward, confident in his inability.

Ensuring he avoided the building surrounded by military trucks, which lay across the to the west, B continued north toward the next house in sight on the east side of the road. The walls of the home were constructed with multicolored mud bricks, bits of red, black, and tan scattered randomly. It was then topped by a few sheets of brown tin, either rusted or severely sun-burned, and a tree stood over the top of the house on the opposite side. It looked like it had at least two or three small rooms. B noticed a window on the side facing him. Wanting to avoid being seen yet to ensure his appearance was strategic, he ducked quickly to the right, moving behind the back of the house and out of sight of this window. As he did so, he noticed just on the other side of the place a garden, just under the tree, with scattered greenery sprouting up from a defined area of dark brown soil. This appeared markedly different from the surrounding land, which was dry and sparse; this garden was clearly tended to and had growth in it. After it came fully into view, he noticed Gideon: he had a tool and appeared to be digging and tending to it somehow.

He watched from the shade of the back of the house, unseen. It seemed Gideon was removing some weeds from the garden. His face was glazed with sweat, and the piercing Congolese sun was bearing down on him.

Then, abruptly, a woman emerged from the house, carrying a burlap bag whose contents were unknown. She approached Gideon quickly in the garden, and he set down his tool and listened to her speak. B was too far away to hear her words, but he could tell she was speaking urgently; her eyes darted to her right and left as she spoke, as if attempting to hide from someone.

Bikonzi knew this was the moment he needed, so he started to walk. Emerging from the shade of the house, he kept his head down and dragged his feet along the ground weakly. As he walked, he ensured his arms remained stuck down, not swaying with his movement. As he stepped into the sun, almost instantaneously, a bead of sweat began to drip from his forehead to his face and body. It fell to the ground, watering the dry dust at his feet.

At first, neither Gideon nor the woman noticed. He continued to commit to the act, however, not diverting his eyes from the ground and ensuring he would be seen as utterly pitiful whenever he was noticed. If she were showing compassion on Gideon, she would surely show compassion on this poor, pitiful boy wandering by. He decided to put on a good show for her - he would get whatever he could from her, even if it meant undermining his cousin. Gideon was stronger anyway; Bikonzi deserved more help. He was fighting for his life here.

Gideon saw him first: the woman's back was to Bikonzi, and Gideon noticed him approach out of his peripherals. His eyes bounced between him and the woman, and though he did his best to hide it on his face, she noticed that something behind her had grabbed his attention, and she turned curiously. B only continued his sad, slow walk, ensuring neither of his feet ever left the ground. It was as if his whole body was weighed by chains.

She still held the burlap sack, and in noticing Bikonzi, spoke to Gideon. As B moved closer, he could hear her voice this time.

"Before I give this to you, you must swear to share this rice with that small boy there as well. Do you promise?"

There was a brief pause from Gideon.

"Will you share with him?" she asked again, this time more sternly.

"Yes. I will share with that boy."

"Good. Eat now while it is warm, and you can finish the garden when you are done."

"Yes, ma'am."

There were no more words; their conversation was followed by her simple footsteps back into the house and then silence.

B now looked up.

Gideon was fuming, staring directly at him. His forehead wrinkled, and his eyebrows scrunched. His fist closed tightly around the top of the burlap bag. With his gaze still fixed on B, he moved promptly to what little shade the tree provided at this point.

Bikonzi smiled slightly and walked over to Gideon in the shade. As he approached, he quoted the woman.

"You heard her - we need to share."

"You didn't work for this; you don't deserve this."

"You heard what she said."

"That doesn't mean I have to. She's back inside now."

"I can go and tell her that you are not sharing the rice."

"That's fine; you'll give yourself away. Besides, by the time you return, I will have eaten this whole bag."

They continued to go back and forth, and B realized he was unlikely to win this argument. He had no power here and was not strong enough to fight Gideon for the bag. As they argued, B noticed a flash of movement beyond Gideon toward the road. Glancing up quickly, he saw Daniel walking by on the other side of the road, presumably looking for food himself. He looked miserable: his bruises had caused him to walk with a limp, and his eye was still a little swollen. Then, without hesitation, Bikonzi responded to Gideon.

"Look, there's Daniel. I can call him over to eat this rice with us."

He hated to use Daniel as a pawn in this way, but he needed some advantage over Gideon's strength. He needed this rice and was committed to getting it any way he could.

Gideon abandoned their argument and looked quickly over his shoulder, spotting Daniel as well. Without hesitation, he grabbed B and scrambled to hide behind the trunk of the tree they stood under. Putting his back against the trunk and holding the burlap bag in one hand, he quickly thrust his other hand to cover Bikonzi's mouth as he sat in front of him.

"You stay quiet, and if you do, I will share this with you. Deal?"

With his mouth covered, B opened his eyes wide and nodded, looking directly at Gideon's face.

"Okay. Now be quiet."

They did not utter a word as Daniel passed by, following the road and continuing to the houses further away.

When he was out of earshot, Gideon shifted his attention to the rice.

"Alright, we will take turns scooping rice from the bag now. I go first."

Gideon plunged his hand into the bag and grabbed as large an amount as his fingers would allow. He shoved the entirety of it into his mouth, expanding his cheeks to fit it all. As he did this, a few grains fell to the side, bouncing off his cheeks and descending into the dirt beneath them. He chewed briefly, returned both hands to the bag, and opened it up for Bikonzi to take a handful.

B reached in and followed suit, grabbing as much as he could and tossing it into his mouth. Gideon continued with his next handful, and Bikonzi with his. Then, Bikonzi became aware that he was getting considerably less rice in this system. His hands were notably smaller than Gideon's, and thus his scoops held less. He kept this in his mind and watched

Gideon carefully, adjusting up into a squatting position while Gideon remained seated and slouched against the tree.

He noticed that, during Gideon's next handful, he gripped the bag with considerably less force, using only three fingers on one hand to pinch the end of it while the other hand dug into the bag. Once Gideon was done with this handful, he returned his second hand to the bag again and held it forward. B took his turn, scooping out his smaller share.

As Gideon reached in for his next turn, he continued the same process, only barely pinching the bag in his hand as he tossed his head back and ate the rice. Then, within the span of less than a second, B swiftly snatched the bag from his hands, turned, and ran. He was beyond the garden in only four strides, his arms pumping quickly to pace his body forward. He heard Gideon yelling behind him, his words interrupted and unintelligible amidst his mouthful of rice. B did not look back but only continued to run.

He continued to hear Gideon's voice chasing him, and as he looked off into the distance for a location to run to, he realized that he would eventually run out of room. There was also no reason for Gideon to stop chasing him, so B began to open the bag and eat while he ran. This proved more difficult than he anticipated, as the bag bounced around with every step, emitting a few grains of rice as he went. They flew up and around him, mixing with the cloud of dust created by his feet. His handfuls were also less substantial, for he could not focus on maximizing the amount he grabbed while running. Gideon continued to chase him, his curses becoming clearer as he swallowed more of the rice in his mouth. His voice grew louder as well, implying to B that he was getting closer, and so he sped up his running scoops, and within a few more attempts he had exhausted the contents of the bag. When he had done so, he immediately dropped it into the dirt, not slowing his sprint in any way.

He heard Gideon's footsteps slow and stop. B used this opportunity to glance over his shoulder, quickly seeing Gideon grab the empty bag, beating dirt from it and terminating his chase. He saw Gideon raise his fist in the air in frustration, remaining quiet for fear of the guards hearing their fight.

Bikonzi turned back, now racing to the room. That was the most food he had eaten since their arrival here and easily the most fun he had had in weeks. His stomach churned after the influx of food, and he felt a bit nauseous. Sweat continued to trickle down his head, and he glanced down and noticed that his big toe was bleeding. He cared little about his sweat or his toe. He cared only that his stomach had been filled. As he ran, a slow and steady smile crept across his face.

CHAPTER 7:
WORK

"Wood already touched by fire is not hard to set alight."

-African Proverb

As he expected, he immediately began to draw the silent ire of Gideon. Since that day, Bikonzi felt eyes burning and bearing down on him, and each time he glanced toward Gideon, he was met by a piercing glare. B's chosen response was one of indifference, attempting never to look toward him or Traya's family, and while he continued to feel their eyes, they did not change his actions.

Following his first instance of success, Bikonzi wasted little time attempting to duplicate this effort. While it was clear to him through the side-eyed glances and furrowed eyebrows of his mother that she did not entirely approve of his actions, the nearness of Death and the lack of explicit condemnation gave him a sort of freedom in his excursions.

The following week, Bikonzi ventured out again, walking along the east side of the road, careful to stay far away from what he presumed must be the military barracks. He passed the first house, which had previously been where Gideon was tending the garden; he heard what sounded like voices inside, but wanting to avoid any repetition of his previous experience, he continued forward. The next house along the roadside was constructed similarly to the first: a thatch roof hanging over mud bricks. This one was considerably smaller, and the edges were rounded rather than squared. There was no discernable break between the earth and the home's walls; it was as if it grew up out of the ground. This house lacked a garden, but noises also arose from inside as he approached. It sounded as if someone was sweeping, and he heard what seemed to be clanging pots and pans.

There were three windows on the north, south, and east sides and a doorway on the west side, facing the road. B moved stealthily to the south wall, ensuring he was out of sight of the window and listened. He did not hear much speaking, only sounds of movement and activity. This lasted for a long while, perhaps an hour, with only scattered words breaking in between sounds of work. After this long wait, it took Bikonzi fifteen minutes to move from crouching to sitting, his back pinned against the warm brick of the house. There was a bit of shade he could sit in, and it moved progressively east with the sun. He inched along with it.

Finally, just as the shade was running out, Bikonzi heard an exchange of words in the place. Their voices were soft and difficult to hear.

"...rice...beans...vegetables. When you're...sit...have..," a female voice said intermittently from the room.

After a brief pause, he heard a response. "Thank you," a boy's voice returned. He could not tell exactly whose it was due to the low volume, but he had heard enough to know there was food was inside of this place.

He elevated himself back to a squat and reevaluated his surroundings. He figured that simply walking into the place would be unacceptable—it would be too bold, and it could imply that he had eavesdropped. He needed to find a way to draw on her sympathy more subtly.

He first tested the windows. Standing just a few inches apart, he found his head peeking just over the bottom of the opening. He could see if he stood on his toes, but he could hardly get relevant attention this way. The doorway would need to be his way in. He moved methodically toward it, scanning the road in both directions for any guards who might be nearby. There were none, and so he started to walk.

Ensuring he was within eyesight of the doorway, around ten or fifteen feet from the entrance and along the edge of the road, he trudged slowly along, eyes aimed strictly at the dirt. He paced methodically and slowly, dragging his feet as he did as if his legs would at any moment give out from under him. He proceeded to a point where he figured he was out of sight of the doorway entirely, around fifty or so feet from where he started. No voices called out from inside the place.

He stopped, turned, and walked back.

He dared not look up at any point. If he made any eye contact, it could imply his intentions, revealing that his happening upon the house was no mere accident but was a calculated endeavor. He remembered times when he had attempted to gain sympathy from other authorities in the past. When a teacher or administrator attempted to sift through the conflict, his sad eyes and downcast spirit would often bring him an advantage, so long as they knew he wasn't faking it. This became harder at home, as his mother seemed to have a sort of piercing vision beyond his outward expressions - she could always tell if his hurt was genuine, but it was clear to him with strangers: if you can get them to believe your suffering, you can get them to relieve it. He needed to make it seem as if the woman in the house was acting completely of her own volition; he knew that her compassion needed to seem ultimately her own and not artificially prompted by his action.

He stopped, turned, and walked back.

He noticed now that sweat began to gather on his forehead. It pooled and dripped down in beads, eventually falling and wetting the dry ground in small droplets of moisture. Some started to pool on his upper lip, and he licked it. Salt shouted at his taste buds, and his jaw clenched slightly at the sudden burst of moisture and flavor in his otherwise dry mouth: fifty more feet and no voices.

He stopped, turned, and walked back.

As he continued, he started to adjust his walk. While his feet dragged, he also ensured his arms ceased swaying. He wanted to make every step look impossible as if the heat could collapse him at any moment. He started to kick the small pebbles and rocks in front of him as well, adding in some noise to grab their attention but avoiding being outright obvious. Fifty more feet and no voices.

He stopped, turned, and walked back.

B continued like this for numerous laps, steadfast in his steps. He counted at first but eventually gave up that endeavor. Eventually, he lost track of where his feigning of fatigue stopped, and real exhaustion set in. Being in direct sunlight at this time of day, with little food and water in his system, left him withered as he went.

Then, after maybe fifteen minutes, he heard a woman's voice call to him.

"You! Boy! Come in here."

He stopped walking and noticed one of his toes had split and was oozing blood. He did not turn his head right away; after walking facing down for so long, he almost forgot how he might need to respond when they actually noticed him. After a few seconds, she called again, potentially unsure if B had heard her.

"Hey! Come in here and eat."

He turned upon this second call and—without smiling—dragged his feet through the doorway and into the home.

The first thing he noticed was the cool air in the place. The transition from sun to shade was a relief, and whatever sweat had not dropped to the ground now started on the work of cooling his body. His eyes took a couple of seconds to adjust to the room before he could take it in.

With his eyes acclimated, he noticed the large rectangular table. It sat in the center of the main room, topped by a collection of baskets. They looked to be made of raffia fibers, strung together in a twill pattern, and each one contained a different food item. Rice, lima beans, and baked sweet potatoes all poked up from the top of each basket, their heat and smell emanating throughout the room. He glanced to his left and noticed the woman in the kitchen area, and it looked to him like she was continuing to prepare even more food. He noticed a doorway to what he presumed to be some sort of bedroom on the other side of the table. It was covered by a curtain, which hung from just above the door nearly to the ground.

Only just then did Bikonzi notice a boy already sitting at the table in front of him. Michael, Fistan's younger brother, sat quietly and stared aggressively at B as he moved toward him. Bikonzi stepped slowly to the seat next to Michael, pulled the chair out from under the table, and quietly sat. Michael's eyes followed him the entire way.

The woman arrived at the table with a bowl of recently washed tomatoes. She seemed hurried and quickly spoke.

"Alright, you both can eat as much of this food as you need. What you do, do quickly."

Bikonzi looked into her eyes as she spoke and saw a kind of desperation. It was clear that she felt this was not allowed for her, and she was doing everything she could to avoid being caught. B couldn't imagine a positive consequence for her actions, yet she had put great effort into ensuring they could eat here, in her home, today.

Driven by instinct for food and slightly out of a desire to ensure he respected the kindness of this woman, B did not hesitate. He immediately grabbed a handful of rice and a sweet potato, eating directly from his hands. They were both still warm and soft, easy to chew and swallow. This aided him greatly, as there was little moisture left in his mouth to help ease the process. The woman left them at the table, disappearing behind the curtained room.

Michael, after seeing her exit, immediately began to verbally dig into Bikonzi.

"What are you doing here?! You didn't work for this!"

B ignored him outright as he ate. A few scattered grains of rice had fallen onto his body and the ground as he feverishly continued to consume as much as he could, as quickly as he could.

"Hey! Listen to me! You shouldn't be eating any of this!"

B now grabbed a tomato and bit into it. Immediately, sweet moisture and an explosion of flavor filled his mouth.

"I can't believe you!"

Michael shoved Bikonzi slightly. B ignored the contact, swaying in his seat from the force as he continued to fill his mouth and stomach.

"This should be mine! I worked for this!"

The sweet potatoes and tomatoes were nearly gone, and B had moved on now to the rice and beans.

The fact that his exclamations were eliciting no response seemed only to infuriate Michael further. He focused his energy more on B, now failing to recognize that the food on the table was nearly entirely exhausted. He shoved B again, harder this time, but having experienced it once before, he rebounded again quickly and persisted in eating.

This energy persisted for a few more minutes, and then the woman returned to the room, forcing Michael to lower his voice. He looked at her as she approached the table, and for the first time, Michael actually examined the food in front of him. The sweet potatoes and tomatoes were completely gone, and a few more beans and grains of rice remained scattered around each of the baskets they had been served in.

"Good!" the woman exclaimed, smiling slightly as she looked at both Michael and Bikonzi. "I'm glad you were able to eat it all!"

She took the baskets and bowls from the table to the kitchen and began to wash them accordingly. B watched her for a moment and then said his first two words since entering the place.

"Thank you."

And then, without making any eye contact with Michael, B pushed his chair out from under himself, turned, and walked to the doorway. His toe stung slightly, but his stomach was full. Michael, again, this time whispering to avoid being heard, protested. Bikonzi did not turn. He wiped tomato and black bean residue from his lips and cheek and stepped out into the sunlight. His eyes squinted as they adjusted, and a smile came across his face as he moved along the roadside. All in a day's work.

CHAPTER 8:
POWER

"If there is no enemy within, the enemy outside can do no harm."

-African Proverb

The compassion of the two women he had interacted with at the camp was a curious thing to Bikonzi. In the midst of a place filled with death and decay, they seemed entirely out of place, willing to care for and sustain them. They had even prompted some of the older boys to bring back food to the rest of the families who remained in the room and thus worked to keep many others alive. Where had such care come from? Why were they doing this? Since they had been taken, no one outside of Bikonzi's family had shown them any real compassion, and he had no frame for this sort of response. He wondered what their stories were.

As the boys had started to work, the security continued to loosen. With the free labor at the camp, the guards and soldiers resorted to simply roaming occasionally, ensuring no one was attempting any escape or otherwise acting out of line. This proved effective because their arrivals to a given house, or to the room, or along the roadside were unpredictable, and each of the boys knew that at any moment, they could be caught in the midst of laziness, stealing, or the like. This more relaxed approach seemed to keep the boys largely on task in their work.

With increased freedom came an increased food supply for all the families. Rice, beans, corn, tomatoes, and mangoes returned with them from their work trips. Initially, this was welcomed, and each family simply ate what their own had brought back; this easy system, though, quickly began to change.

Late one afternoon, after David and Christian had returned to feed their younger siblings with the spoils of their effort, Traya approached them. B hadn't noticed her during the day; she had been sitting in the darkest corner of the room for hours, avoiding the sunbeams pouring in through the broken windows, but now she stood slowly from her seat against the cold concrete wall on the south side, moving into his peripherals. He turned to watch her approach: her eyes were small and focused, and a toothless smirk crept across her face as she moved toward the boys.

B glanced from her back to Christian and David. They distributed handfuls of rice to Ana and Amani, their two remaining younger siblings, who gladly wolfed them down. There was a clear tenderness to them; Christian had squatted down as he carefully handed out the food, avoiding any excess spills or waste of grains. David was assisting in the effort, running his fingers through the short and frayed hair of his siblings and speaking softly to them as they ate. The arrival of Traya to the boys abruptly interrupted their work. She spoke with an authority that forced them to listen.

"It must be difficult trying to care for these poor children by yourselves…" she started.

This comment was not met with any reaction; Christian and David simply continued in their work, refraining from even turning their heads to acknowledge her.

B stood quietly and moved from the west to the north wall, adjacent to the conversation, to better hear.

"I'm sure you miss your mother…" she stated.

She feigned compassion as she spoke, and it became clear that her words said more than her words. Still no reaction from the boys.

"And that poor child... what was his name?" she continued.

At this, Christian turned his head slowly, taking a deep breath as his eyes stared coldly into hers. He did not speak.

"It would be a shame for these two to end up like..." she said as she looked directly into Christian's eyes.

Before she had concluded her sentence, Christian lunged at her, a dry and guttural screech emerging from his hands as he reached for her. At this point, the rest of the room had turned, taking in the scene unfolding before them. Traya jumped back initially, but the speed with which she raised her hands and caught him in his lunge implied that she had anticipated his action. Her words clearly intended to spark it.

She caught him by the wrists, stumbling back slightly as she slowed his momentum. She then reversed it, forcing the boy backward and down, back first, into the concrete floor. She hung over him, her face straining and veins bulging as she restrained his movement. Christian's face shifted, morphing from anger to fear as he realized he had been overpowered. After a few brief seconds, she spoke again.

"Those guards are stronger than I am. You're going to need someone who can protect you, who can provide for you. Your mother failed you, but I won't. Stay with me and my family, and I will keep you safe."

The changes in tone from Traya were jarring to Bikonzi. In one moment, she seemed compassionate; in another, manipulative. He reflected back on that first night they were taken, huddled tightly together with his family. He remembered hearing her voice first, a distant call from the dark night before chaos broke in. And again, he wondered why it was *that* night, that specific time when his father was home, that the guards knew to arrive and capture him. They had failed numerous times prior; what finally led them to him? How did they know he was there? Seeing Traya like this now, a sort of split personality jockeying for her own way, ultimately made him wonder for the first time: had she led them there? Had her voice of urgency been borne of this same conflict she now embodied in front of him—this tension between caring for their family and saving her own skin? He could hardly make sense of this notion in his head that someone could be two things like that. His mind hurt.

After finishing her words, she stared again at him. After his body had relaxed and his resistance settled, she released him and walked back to her darkened corner, sitting with her children. No one spoke. Bikonzi's eyes followed her back, and upon sitting down, she stared out of the darkness. B only saw her eyes, piercing the dusk of the room and directing themselves to him. He felt a shiver, and he quickly turned away.

Only a few days later, Christian and David had already moved to Traya's corner of the room, functionally expanding her family and food resources. Any rewards from Christian and David's work would now be shared with the rest of Traya's family, including Gideon. While B was not positive about how the food rations were divided amongst them, he could not imagine that Christian and David would receive fair portions from their work. Yet they had little choice: they had no power in the place.

It would seem that this would be enough for Traya: additional food rations that she could use for herself and her family. Her power, however, did not keep within the bounds of her southern corner of the room; it moved to conquer again. One morning, as the sun began to heat up, she slowly and methodically moved across the room to Fistan.

Fistan's mother, Mary, had witnessed Christian's overtaking before, and she was well aware of the woman's motives. Thus, Mary moved closely behind Fistan; B noticed her eyebrows squinting into an aggressive skepticism as she approached. Traya's eyes focused narrowly on Fistan, avoiding even acknowledging Mary. Once she was within arm's reach, she began.

"You know, your mother can't take care of you, son…"

Mary's facial expression shifted, now into a robust glare. She did not, however, fight back, which confounded Bikonzi. Why would she let her say such things? He felt the urge to jump forward in anger—how could she hold back such rage?

Fistan did not reply, so Traya continued.

"She can't. You will see - she is going to end up like the other woman from before," she said as she pointed to the now-empty northeast corner of the room where Eden and Abel had formerly been.

Fistan again remained silent, but his eyes were focused strictly on Traya. He briefly licked his lips, which were cracked and slightly bloody at the corners, but he remained unphased.

"Don't believe me? Look at your younger siblings. Their bodies will tell you all you need to know."

B involuntarily followed this command himself, examining the rest of Fistan's family. Fistan's younger siblings—Clarice, Titi, and Marcelin—lay on the ground. Two of them groaned, and all of them laid down, quiet and lethargic. Though the room had received an influx of food, it fell well short of the nutrients needed to fully sustain them. His older sisters, Mamie and Esther, sat adjacent to the littlest ones, watching the conversation intently and sleepily. It was clear they were drained of energy themselves: throughout their time in the camp so far, the older girls focused mainly on helping their mothers with the littlest in the room. Carrying, soothing, waking in the middle of the night, helping them to sleep and stay clean amid their malnourishment—they were extensions of their mothers' care to their siblings. Between their sleeplessness and constant exposure to the horrors of unhealth in their midst, their fatigued faces made sense to Bikonzi at this moment.

"That's enough!" Mary suddenly exclaimed, "This is my family!"

She began to move in front of Fistan, attempting to force Traya to address her directly. Just as she moved in between, however, a swift and unexpected palm landed squarely across her face.

The sharp and loud smack echoed off the bare concrete walls. Mary immediately collapsed, falling to the ground. As she lay down, she looked back up at Traya, mouth wide and eyes staring in disbelief. An eyes-wide glare met her, tightened lips, and strained cheeks, which then slowly turned back to Fistan.

"You see? She cannot protect you. She is frail. She is scared."

B noticed tears now running down Mary's face. She did not speak a word, and her mouth now trembled as she observed the situation.

He glanced back at Fistan now. His head was still turned toward his siblings and now pivoted to his mother. They held their gaze, both their eyes watering. Then Fistan began to shake his head, wiping his face with his arm as he did. He turned back to Traya and responded.

"Okay. You're right. We need you to protect us."

It was only now that Bikonzi realized he had been holding his breath for the last few seconds. He released the captive air and watched again as his Traya smiled, first at Fistan and then at Mary. She spoke again now.

"Good. You have made the right choice. Bring your family to my corner of the room. Leave your mother."

Fistan nodded to the rest of his siblings, and they promptly followed Traya as ordered.

She had now conquered three-fourths of the room. Bikonzi knew they would be next.

Mary cowered alone in the southwest corner of the room, exhausted and hungry. She had watched as her children had been ripped away from her, and since that day, she had hardly moved from her location. Bikonzi could hear her tears from time to time through the night.

Given that the entire room had watched her manipulation over the course of the last week or so, everyone knew it was only a matter of time until she attempted to take them over as well. John had spoken to B and Moses for the last few nights about how they needed to be ready for this.

"She is coming for Mom," he said plainly two nights earlier as they started to fall asleep. "We need to make sure she doesn't succeed. We can't back down."

Moses and B silently nodded; they knew it would largely be up to John, the oldest male in the family, to lead any level of resistance. B wondered if John was really trying to prepare himself and Moses or prepare himself.

As beads of sweat gathered on her face and the concrete floor warmed in the unshaded portions of the room, Traya again walked her way over to the Moise corner. This time, however, she went directly for Rose. As she walked, B moved his gaze to John to see what he might do. He sat, knees up and crouched against the wall, his fingers fidgeting with some unknown substance. His eyes were cast down as if the rest of the room did not exist. B wondered how he would respond. Turning back to Traya, he discovered she had already come face-to-face with his mother.

"You've seen what has happened the last few days," she said, turning over her shoulder and back to the extended family she had added.

Rose spoke nothing. She simply stared into her eyes, tilting her head slightly as if searching for something.

"You're pregnant. There's no way you can care for these children. You may not even make it through pregnancy. Don't you care about your children?"

Still no response, just an unwavering stare from Rose.

"At this point, the best thing you can do is allow me to take care of them."

Rose avoided any response.

After a short pause, she continued: "You know you cannot take care of that baby." As she said these words, she raised her hand and grabbed Rose's shoulder.

B noticed out of his peripheral vision that John had looked up from his seat and was now watching intently. His head was tilted down, sweat had gathered on his forehead, and he stared intensely at Traya.

"You can't even raise these children. How can you think to bring one more to this world?"

She began to squeeze her hand, tightening it on Rose's shoulder. Still, Rose did not look up, though she flinched slightly in pain.

Everything from there happened almost too quickly for B to recognize. Traya lifted her hand from Rose's shoulder and raised it into the air as if priming herself to strike her face as she did Mary's. At the same time, in an urgent blur, John sprung forward from his place on the wall and grabbed Traya's wrist before it could move any closer to Rose. She, for the first time in days, had been frozen.

At first, she resisted John's strength, her arm quaking as she attempted to free herself from his grasp. She stared into his eyes, which were unbroken from hers, a silent and unmoving rage radiating from them both. Realizing that she would not overpower John, she gave up her resistance; only then did John release her from his grasp. She rubbed her wrist and slinked backward slightly, and John spoke for the first time.

"If you ever lay a finger on her—if you even look at her wrong—you had better hope that I am not around."

Bikonzi felt his heart leap in his chest as John responded and spoke. He had waited for someone to do something—someone strong and bold enough—to keep Traya from continuing her tyranny. He felt he wasn't big or strong enough to do it, but he knew someone must. And though he so hated his dependency and had put such concerted effort into resisting it, he found himself now deeply grateful for John's presence and strength. He drew closer to his mother, closing his fists tightly and shaking them subtly and firmly in aggressive celebration.

They now stood. John's feet were planted firmly between his mother and Traya. She continued slowly, stepping away, responding as she did.

"You'd better watch out, boy. You'll end up like your father."

John's eyes widened for a brief moment and then furrowed in anger, and he stepped quickly to her.

"You know nothing of my father!" he spoke sternly, holding his right arm up, stepping toward her as if ready to strike.

She sped up her retreat from him, holding her hands above her face in defense and slithering back into her corner. After a couple of steps, John stopped his advance and stood for a few moments until she had finally sat among her children and the others. He wiped the sweat from his brow and turned back to Rose. He hugged her and then silently returned to his sitting spot on the wall.

CHAPTER 9:
PRAYER

"In the moment of crisis, the wise build bridges, and the foolish build dams."

-African Proverb

The sparse and pale moonlight shone into the place in spurts, its beams radiant and defined against the black backdrop of the room. Everyone had settled down for the night, doing their best to drift off to sleep following the heightened tension of recent days. Crickets chirped, and trees rustled as the earth began to sleep.

As Bikonzi began to fall into a half-sleep, his body jerked him awake at an abrupt break in the noise of the night. Soft, urgent whispers sprung into earshot, emerging above the natural noise of the night. B dared not move but strained his ears to listen; his eyes remained closed to remain solely focused on listening.

He discerned they were arising from Traya's corner of the room, three or four voices speaking indiscernibly. There was one female voice, which he presumed to be Traya's, and three male voices responding and listening.

Then, without warning, they abruptly paused. Silence filled the room for a few minutes, and the crickets re-emerged to their rightful place in the nightly soundtrack. As B rolled over and resumed his attempt to sleep, though, he heard the light shuffling of feet upon the concrete floor. The steps were slow, growing louder over the proceeding seconds. They were moving toward him.

His mind darted between paralysis and action. In one sense, his current position was the safest he could be; he sat just a few feet away from John, who would surely awaken in the event of his family being threatened. More than that, the element of surprise could prove beneficial, as he could jump up and away if they did not expect him to be awake in the first place. He simultaneously felt the urge to spring up to his feet now and wake John and Moses so that they might be best prepared for what was to come. But what was to come?

The steps continued, creeping closer to the Moises. B clenched his hands and feet, straining his muscles in tension, awaiting any circumstance. His eyes were wide open now, facing opposite the sounds he heard. A beam of moonlight was cast in front of him, illuminating John's legs in the night. Suddenly, a leg landed inches in front of his face. Then, two more legs. Soon, he saw the backs of four boys emerging, passing directly by him and moving toward John. Their shadowy presence remained unidentifiable for Bikonzi, and he simply watched as they continued their methodical movement.

Two of them circled around John, passing through the moonlight briefly and turning as they did. This exposed Gideon and his brother, Cain, for a brief moment. The other two boys remained with their backs to B. They stared down, and John then moved their heads back up toward one another. They nodded and glanced back downward.

Before their eyes locked back onto John, he sprung upward and onto his feet. They were startled by this, jumping back slightly. John now clearly stood in the moonlight, his eyes bouncing amongst the four boys that surrounded him. They stood and paused only briefly before Gideon made the first move. He swung a fist at John's face, which he ducked narrowly to avoid, disappearing into the darkness and reemerging into the moonlight.

He swung quickly into Gideon's body, landing a fist in his gut and pushing him backward slightly.

The other three boys rallied to tackle John from here, knocking all of them further into the darkness. It was a shadowy mob of grunts and growls at this point, and Gideon rejoined the fray after recovering from his stumble. B sat up slightly, leaning on his elbow. He was concerned for John but also knew he was too small to jump into the fight and be of assistance. The tension of his dependency arose again in his heart: he hated his smallness again. Others around the room slowly awoke to the noise, turning their attention toward the fight.

The mob of boys began to move, rolling across the floor and breaking in and out of the light as they did. Occasionally, a boy would be tossed aside, only to re-engage again. From what B could tell, John remained in the middle, attempting to fight off these four boys as he did.

The first real smack came a couple of minutes into the fight. Though he did not see the punch clearly, B could hear it; it was short and sharp, quickly disappearing into the night air. A boy stumbled back and fell face-down a few feet away, groaning and rolling over. Given that the other boys continued, B presumed that John was still in the fight.

It took a couple of minutes for the next boy to fall. He was tackled down and back, smacking his shoulder blades into the moonlit concrete. John was upon him immediately, and two swift punches to the face forced him to roll over and protect his body. The two remaining boys grabbed John and tossed him back into the darkness.

The next boy fell as his legs were swept out from under him. B saw the outline of his body lift entirely off the ground and then crumble down again, rolling in pain as he landed. John remained standing.

There was a lull in combat as the remaining boy and John circled around each other, their arms protecting each of their faces. They both passed in and out of the light, exposing bloodied and bruised faces. Bikonzi watched in wonder at the strength of his brother. Though he was older than the rest of these boys, he was just as malnourished - yet he fought with remarkable endurance. John had always been that way:

steadfast, unrelenting, driven. He rarely lost in their neighborhood soccer games - his physicality was always matched by mental intensity, pushing him further than anyone else. As all bodies failed here, including his, Bikonzi felt it must have been something in his mind, spirit, and will that separated him now.

B realized that Gideon was left as his face lit up in the passing moonlight. He wore a concerned expression, his eyebrows angled upward, and his mouth pursed. After seeing the other three fall, it had seemed to settle in for him: this fight was unlikely to be won.

On the other hand, John displayed focus, his eyes bearing in upon Gideon as he tilted his head down. Confidence oozed alongside his bloody nose.

Then suddenly, without warning, John drove his body into Gideon, lowering his shoulder into his chest and driving him to the ground. An audible release of air arose as he crashed down, and John landed three punches before sitting up and pausing over him. Gideon had gone limp, his head rolling to the side. He breathed only slightly and began to curl himself and roll over onto his side. John now stood, wiping his face as he did. The four boys slowly gathered together and limped their way back to the corner of the room.

John remained standing, watching and listening until he heard them settle. He turned away, stepped back toward the moonlight, and laid down.

Crickets chirped, and trees rustled as the earth returned to sleep.

Daylight swiftly revealed the cost of that night. Gideon and Cain seemed to take the worst of it; both had eyes swollen shut and bruises already darkening on their shoulders. Michael and Fistan were hurt as well, sitting crumpled on the floor for most of the following days.

John was not without blemish: his lower lip was swollen, the whites of his eyes were strained red, and he also had scattered bruises across his body. No words were spoken between the boys themselves.

Rose was concerned but unsurprised upon waking and finding the damage done to John. She and Amiee comforted him, providing him with some additional water the next morning as he recovered. Given the beaten conditions of those five boys, it remained up to others in the families to work and produce food for the group. Moses, Christian, and David thus set out on this day, and after hanging back and allowing them to begin their work, Bikonzi followed. He hoped to continue in the strategy that had proven so effective for him previously, seemingly stumbling upon food right as it was being given away.

It took him a few minutes to discover where the other boys had proceeded to but again found himself benefitting from fortunate timing. In the third house on the east side of the road, just before it curved west toward the homes of the commanders, he heard voices emerging from inside. Walking along the road, he peeked in to find all the boys sitting beside one another, spread out evenly and surrounding a large table. A woman had hurriedly commenced setting the table with bowls and pans, the contents of which he could not see.

B quickly evaluated the situation. Though he knew that casually passing by and waiting to be noticed had worked previously, this woman seemed too preoccupied in this instance. More than that, if he had to wait a bit, he may not end up with much food, for the rest of the boys may consume the majority of it. He thus opted to boldly enter the house and simply join them at the table.

After passing through the doorway, Christian was the first to notice him. He sat at the end of the table while the other two boys sat with their backs to the doorway.

"What are you doing here?!" Christan asked.

Bikonzi silently circled the table, pulled out a chair, and climbed onto it opposite Moses and David, who had now turned and watched him join.

"B, you shouldn't be here," Moses declared.

"Why not?" he responded, "The door was open."

The woman returned to the table, and a pot full of rice and beans arrived. She noticed B, glancing quickly at him but not directly addressing him. She spoke now to all of them.

"You need to hurry. My husband will be home at any moment."

She left the table again and swiftly returned to the kitchen, bringing back yams topped with honey and lemon peel, kachumbari, a tomato dish mixed with avocado and red onion, and a pan full of green sauce poured over small pieces of chicken.

Hearing her urgency, Bikonzi began to reach into the bowl of rice, but before he could touch it, a swift smack landed upon his hand from Moses.

"We are going to thank God before we eat," he said plainly.

Bikonzi stared at him in confusion and annoyance.

"Pray? Did you hear her? We need to eat! He could be home at any moment," he rebutted as he reached again for the food.

Again, Moses's hand landed upon B's, grabbing and holding it tightly now.

"We will pray," he said sternly, tossing Bikonzi's hand back at him.

In astonishment, B slowly moved his hand away, his frustration brewing and clear upon his face. Pray to what? God certainly wasn't here, at this camp or at this table, and even if he were, he wasn't very interested in listening or helping.

He looked at Christian and David, who both simply avoided eye contact with Moses, bowing their heads slightly. B could not believe this was happening. He turned back to Moses, who was glaring at him, waiting for him to close his eyes and bow his head in conjunction with the others. Resentfully, and keeping his eyes glared across the table at his brother, he lowered his head and closed his eyes. A few seconds later, Moses began.

"Dear Father God, thank you…" he started.

Thank you? Bikonzi had started to understand why people like Moses and Christian kept their faith here: though he didn't feel God was anywhere near them, to hope in something like God made sense to him. But to say '*Thank you*' to him in prayer? That seemed a bit too far. After all, what was there really to be thankful for? This meal was only the result of their creative work—this food hadn't just dropped from the sky. And furthermore, if they waited much longer, there wouldn't be any food left to be thankful for anyway! The words 'Thank you' had never stung so sharply, and they prompted B to pen one eye and peek at his peers. Everyone else kept their eyes closed while Moses continued. They all seemed to follow Moses' lead. Whether or not they really believed didn't matter to him; they, too, could cost all of them precious food.

Slowly, keeping his eyes open and head swiveling around the room, B quickly grabbed a handful of rice and beans and shoved them into his mouth. They were hot, and he felt his tongue burning as he ate. He swallowed quickly, and the food warmed his throat and chest as it went down.

"Thank you for the many ways you have blessed us, even now…"

As the words continued, so did Bikonzi: he snatched a tomato and bit into it. His brother could have all the faith he wanted; he needed to eat. Juice popped from the fruit as he did, forcing David to peek his eye open at the noise. He noticed Bikonzi eating during the prayer and glanced slightly at Moses. Bikonzi shook his head urgently, his eyes widening as he continued to eat. David turned himself slightly back down and closed his eyes again.

"Thank you for all of this food…"

On to the yams went B, feverishly consuming everything he could. He felt a tinge of guilt creep in as he ate what was meant to be shared by all, but ultimately, it was their fault. They chose to pause in this way—they had every right to eat as much as he did. He noticed his hands start to get messy, and the floor below him showed evidence of his rushed eating.

"In Jesus name, amen…" Moses finished.

After he finished his prayer, footsteps thudded outside. The woman who fed them turned from the kitchen, glancing briefly at the boys as she looked back to the front doorway. Her eyes bulged, and the boys knew without her words that they needed to leave.

The sound of boots entered the place, and all of the boys looked up at the man who entered. He was tall, wiry, dressed in a long-sleeved khaki jacket. He wore sunglasses, which he quickly removed as his eyes adjusted to the cool, dark air inside. As he removed the glasses, he exposed confused and angry eyes, which scanned over the boys swiftly.

They sat silently, paralyzed by the moment.

"What are they doing here?!" the man yelled, increasing his volume with each word.

Without hesitation he moved toward the table, and the boys each scattered like ants from a stomping foot. B managed to grab a last handful of rice and shove it into his mouth alongside the yams already present; his cheeks bulged as he scooted around the other end of the table. Out of desperation, Christian grabbed the entire pot of green sauce, snatching it away and quickly following Bikonzi across to the other end of the table. Moses and David jumped out of the way of the man, who now grasped the edge of the table. With a roar, he flipped the entire thing over, food flying and crashing onto the ground.

"I would rather the rats eat this than them!" he said.

Pots clanged against the ground, and tears could be heard from the kitchen as the man's wife watched helplessly. As he flipped this table, the boys did not wait to see what happened next. Within seconds, they were out the door, sprinting back to the room.

"What were you thinking?!" they heard the man yell in the distance.

They stumbled over one another as they ran, their arms and legs flailing frantically as they fled. Christian and David scooped hot handfuls of the sauce and chicken, splattering the liquid onto the ground and their faces as well as into their mouths. After they had exhausted themselves, Christian simply dropped the pot into the middle of the road and focused on running the rest of the way.

After a minute more, as they approached the room, they each looked back and found no one was chasing them. They slowed to a walk, allowing their lungs and pulses to slow. No one spoke.

B examined the other boys. Christian's shirt and face were splattered with sauce, and he licked his lips, attempting to gather any other flavor he could. David's chest expanded and contracted rapidly, and he licked his fingers with food residue. He looked to Moses, whose eyes were cast down and whose face remained expressionless.

He had not gotten any food.

CHAPTER 10: RESISTANCE

"A man who uses force is afraid of reasoning."

-African Proverb

Bikonzi awoke in a sweat, his mind rushing with conscious awareness as his dreams emptied his mind like water being poured out of a jar. He was already losing the dream as he caught his breath. There was an unseen ghost he was fleeing, unable to find safety; he ran from home to home to hide, yet upon arrival, each door was locked. He laid back down with his eyes now open, filled with a smattering of both moonlight and darkness of the room.

As the dream slipped away, more thoughts replaced it. It was surprising that he had awakened tonight, as he had found sleep to be more effective the last few days. He attributed this to the influx of food they had received in recent days and weeks; with more nourishment came better rest. He had also felt more secure amidst his family recently. Given the recent colonization of the room by Traya, their family had grown much closer as they attempted to fight her authority as best as they knew how. Moses and John continued to work in the place, trading places as they did so to ensure at least one of them remained in the room when the other was absent.

The family also elected to sleep close together each night, sometimes even interlocking arms. They had become more of a unit in the midst of their fractured world. B closed his eyes as he reflected on this growth.

Then, abruptly, he felt his leg begin to tickle slightly. He thought it might be a brief breeze or a fly, so he swatted at it and scratched briefly. Just a few seconds later, it returned, and he had the same response; he turned and adjusted his body without opening his eyes. Yet again, the feeling returned, and he knew it couldn't just be a fly. He thought it might be Daniel, who had been sleeping amongst the Moises in recent days, either accidentally or intentionally brushing up alongside him.

"Daniel," he whispered, "Stop! I'm trying to sleep."

The tickle remained. It felt like hair brushing up against his leg.

"I'm serious! Daniel, stop messing with me."

It became more forceful, and B felt a hand wrapping around his calf. He flipped his body around to where he felt the hand, yelling as he did.

"Daniel! Stop…" he started, quickly stopping as he took in what had actually been causing the annoyance.

Looming above his feet stood a shadowy figure, his outline prominent as he blocked the moonlight through the broken window. B could see that he had a gun draped around him, and he had now gotten a grasp on his foot and was attempting to drag him away. Without thinking, he screamed as loud as he could.

"Help!"

Rose was the first to rise upon hearing this. She quickly sprung toward B. She shoved the guard back, who stumbled and laughed slightly as she did. Then she grabbed B by his arm tightly and created a chain amongst the other children in her family. John and Moses were now awake, and they continued the chain, linking with their younger siblings as well.

After stumbling back, the guard walked forward again. His steps were wide and inconsistent, and his body wiggled without a solid foundation. He looked drunk.

"You have to do what I say..." he said to Rose. He reached again for B's leg, falling down as he did. 'What was he here to do?' Bikonzi thought as he wriggled away. 'What does he want with me?'

"Not when it comes to my children," Rose responded, reinforcing her grip on her family.

The guard again attempted to drag B by his legs; he continued to scream, weaving his arm tightly with Rose's, preventing little progress from being made at taking him. Both sides strained, and the volume level continued to increase as the Moises cried out alongside B. This human tug-of-war continued for a few seconds before the guard's grip slipped. He awkwardly stumbled backward, nearly falling into the hard concrete wall. As he gathered himself, no words were spoken; Moises sat in silent anticipation as he stood once again. He stared down at the family for a few long seconds, focusing his attention on Amiee specifically, and then walked wordlessly out the door and into the night.

Following a few frantic breaths, the family collapsed, releasing their grips to rest. No one spoke for a few moments. B looked up to the ceiling, his limbs splayed out and exhausted. His elbow and knee were pulsing from the pressure, and his heartbeat remained rapid. As the adrenaline slowed, Rose spoke.

"This won't be the last time they try this."

Rose followed this insight with a groan as she laid her body back down slightly. She was getting bigger. Over the course of the preceding months, her body had become increasingly disproportionate; while continuing to lose needed muscle, her belly continued to expand. She remained sick, and while she attempted to vomit out of the sight of her children and in secret, it was sometimes sudden and unavoidable.

Following this, the family gathered themselves tightly together again. Some of them interlocked arms, while others laid on top of one other; they piled close. Not only did they fight division from within the room. They now knew that they must oppose the greedy hands of the night.

Rose was right. The next few weeks were characterized by regular visits from at least one guard. Sometimes, the visits were loud and careless, with guards stumbling in and finding themselves resisted and pushed out. Other nights, they were more strategic, and the families wouldn't even wake up.

Sleep became even more difficult during this time for the families. The subtlest sound, the lightest noise, would wake them; the rustle of birds and trees startled them out of sleep as if their lives were at risk. B would often wake up without having strung together for more than an hour or two of sleep the night before, and thus, he would be forced to nap during the day to compensate. This also affected the work of the rest of the boys: with less sleep, they proved less capable of the jobs provided to them and more exhausted upon their completion. While the wives remained compassionate with food, the boys were nevertheless regularly returning exhausted.

It was an evening not long after the first that B was awakened again to noise. He was startled up, straining his ears as he moved to sit. The night was still initially, but soon, sounds arose slightly in the distance. He heard multiple sets of footsteps outside the room, quiet at first but growing louder the more he listened. There were urgent, muffled voices, and he heard the mechanical cracking of guns as they walked. They were getting closer, and it sounded as if they would enter the room soon. B crawled quickly to awaken Moses and, in doing so, saw that John and Rose had already woken and were gathering the family together again. They braced for what would come next, though they did not know what it would look like.

Boots burst through the doorway first, crunching as they carried dirt from outside onto the dry concrete. Two of the guards who routinely took the night shifts at the warehouse looked urgently around the place: one was stout, with a pouting expression suspicious of all he took in, his mustache bending downward as he frowned in focus, while the other stood a few inches taller, his thin face amplified by sunken cheekbones. Both were armed with AK-47s, and their eyes and weapons were illuminated by the slivers of moonlight that poured in. B recognized one of them as the man who had come to drag him out of the room those weeks earlier.

After scanning, they both landed specifically upon Amiee. They moved swiftly to her, and John and Moses jumped in between their sister and the men. They were promptly grabbed by the arm and cast aside, feeling the butt of a gun landing into each of their backs as they landed. Just as they reached for Amiee to take her, Rose jumped in front of the men, tears running down her face and hands held high, with her palms facing them.

Taken aback, they stopped their progress briefly, but rather than physically casting Rose aside, they stepped back and barked a command at her.

"Move!" they exclaimed together.

Rose gave no response, only maintaining eye contact, glancing quickly between the two men.

"We said move!" they yelled again.

"I will not move," Rose said quietly and directly.

The guards, confused by this rebuttal, looked quickly at one another and then back at her. One of them raised his weapon upward, pointing it inches from Rose's face.

"Move, or we will shoot you!" he said aggressively.

John and Moses jumped forward at this, and the other guard directed his weapon to each, commanding them to sit down. There was no noise for a few moments, and B sat silently. Tears welled up in his eyes as he stared into the face of his mother. He had always known that Death was near, but it had not yet struck his own family. He held his breath and could not feel his heart. He felt his stomach starting to churn.

The silence was broken by the click-click cocking of the rifle, which the man now steadied.

"I will shoot you!" he reminded Rose.

"If you shoot me, you ease my pain."

The guard was visibly surprised by her response. A few seconds passed as he processed the comment. He lowered the gun and squinted his eyes slightly as he tried to grasp the gall of this woman.

He turned his head slowly back to the other guard who had entered with him, and their eyes met in equal confusion. They had not planned on this sort of resistance; they had come intending to take someone away with them alive, and now, to do that, they'd need to actively take away a second and third life along with it. Bikonzi wondered why it was essential for them to take her away now—what did they need her for? Why were they so aggressive, specifically about her and not anyone else? The actions of these soldiers continued to confuse him.

After a brief pause, the first guard scowled and stormed back out toward the doorway, followed again by his partner. They were gone as quickly as they had arrived.

Rose and Amiee immediately embraced, and the rest of the family again surrounded them. Bikonzi rushed in to hug Rose, who wrapped her arms around him gently. While it became clear to him that Death still reigned here, it was nice to be able to fight back every once in a while.

CHAPTER 11:
BIRTH

"Let your love be like the misty rain,
coming softly but flooding the river."
-African Proverb

A sort of solemnity had gradually overtaken Rose, especially in the last few days. She moved slowly, woke with grimaces, and appeared resigned to the family. Even when some larger quantities of food had been brought back by John, Moses, and the others, she would rarely react beyond serving as a distributor for her children. Smiles, already infrequent, had ceased entirely. Following the family's collective consumption of rice and beans, it was late one afternoon that B noticed this trend.

"Mom?" he inquired, his voice emanating an innocence that hid his recognition of the somber tone she carried with her.

"Yes, my love?" she responded.

She slowly shifted her body to him, her face twisting in pain slightly as she did.

"I have a question."

"Yes?"

B only now realized he wasn't sure exactly what he wanted to ask, and the question emerged unfiltered.

"Why aren't you happy about the baby?" he asked.

After hearing this, Rose's eyes shifted. No longer looking at B, she darted them down, flicking them ever so slightly back and forth as if the answer was somehow to be found on the cold, dark ground. A few seconds passed, and Rose returned her gaze to his eyes.

"My son…" she said.

Her eyes were beginning to flutter and well. She raised her arm to him, grazing his head and settling her hand upon his cheek and neck.

"My body is in pain. I do not know what is coming, for me or for us."

The short sentences came out with pauses in between, as she seemed to be collecting her thoughts and filing them down.

"It seems unfair…"

Her voice trailed off, and her eyes trailed briefly with them before returning to B. In the midst of their shared gaze, he started to see his mother differently, perhaps for the first time. She was not someone who had all of the answers he needed. She was not the person with unending strength and response for him and his family. She was, just as much as anyone else in that room, tattered and afraid.

After a few seconds of silence, B warmly embraced her, curling himself into her arms and resting his head on the top of her belly. With his ear pinned, he could hear a steady sound of compressions, faint but present. His mother's arms formed a canopy upon his back, and for those brief moments, he felt comforted.

Soon after they had eaten, Bikonzi and his family watched the sunset and commenced with their sleep structure, laying down and linking together as best as possible. Rose lay parallel to the west wall, adjacent to Amiee, bracketed by Moses and John. B lay between the closest door and his younger siblings, creating a buffer that would allow for them to be shielded both by John and Moses on one side and by him on the other. They formed a sort of chain of connection, at least one body part in connection or touching with another family member, and many of them with arms linked.

The night descended upon them and was filled with a variety of noises. B tossed throughout, never opening his eyes but regularly shifting his body. He wasn't able to find consistent rest, hearing deep blows of thunder and the steady pitter-patter of rain onto and into the building. The open window frames prevented nothing from entering the room that wanted to, and a pool of water had begun to build a few feet away. He heard, at times, voices indiscernible underneath the noise of the weather. He had fallen in and out of a dream in this time, waking and re-arriving in his unconscious mind.

It had begun in a deep and dark jungle, so thick with trees that the sky had been blocked out entirely. B found himself traversing through it, and though there was no explicit threat, his mind felt an ominous presence near him as he walked. He looked down as he carefully stepped, attempting to avoid noise from the unknown threat. As his gaze shifted, he noticed in his peripheral gaze what appeared to be two feet poking out from behind a short bush to his right. His anxiety increased, and though he only wanted to keep moving and find an escape from the jungle, he was drawn toward the feet as if pulled by a string.

As he arrived at the bush, he saw a fuller body revealed: a man, unmoving and lying on his back. Suddenly, rain began to pour, streaming down his face; thunder clapped all around him. His eyes slowly scanned the man who laid on the ground, starting from his legs and moving forward toward his head. Arriving at his face, he was encountered by a strange confusion: he had a realization, in his mind, that this body was his father's, and yet his face somehow did not match. His father appeared far younger than he remembered; his hair was free from any silver specks, and his forehead was without wrinkle. His eyes were closed, and his chest unmoving, but there were no apparent signs of violence. It was as if he were sleeping without breath.

The moment of strange realization was interrupted swiftly by a distant sound out in the jungle around him. B quickly sprung into a run, looking back once briefly to his father, and upon returning his gaze in front of him, now realized he was running in a shallow stream. His legs splashed about as he moved, and he heard the noises growing louder behind him. The water made it harder to run as if his feet were made of concrete, and his energy became more frenetic. In the midst of his struggle, he heard his mother's voice between continued strokes of thunder, quiet and distant but distinct.

"Nzambe," she called, the word for God in Lingala.

The stream he ran in seemed to be leading toward her voice, and he followed. The volume increased as he struggled closer, and this time, she sounded more desperate, as if she were yelling.

"Nzambe!" she spoke again.

The unknown threat had drawn itself closer, and B now heard footsteps. He dared not look back, his eyes focused forward upon the voice he heard. It seemed the closer he drew to his mother's voice, the closer that presence drew to him until they were both nearly upon him. The sound of his violent splashing filled his ears. His breathing increased, nearly drowning out his mother's voice. Another strike of thunder sounded loudly.

B awoke with a gasp, his lungs filling deeply with the humid air around him. His senses returned to him, starting with his hearing. Rain continued to patter, yet more calmly now. His eyes blinked away their sleep, filled by the faint blue light of dawn pouring in through the open windows. B turned his head slightly while feeling for his siblings. Seth remained where he had remembered them and was sleeping peacefully. He glanced up to where John and Moses had gone to sleep but noticed they were not lying on the ground. He quickly turned his body, concerned that they had been taken, but saw them huddled in the northwest corner of the room.

Confused, he stood and started toward them, scooping Jay and bringing her with him. As he drew closer he saw that his older brothers were shielding Rose and Amiee as well. The boys squatted, tightly compacting their family unit, while Rose and Amiee appeared to be holding something in each of their hands. Upon arriving to the corner of the room, B rested his hands upon the shoulders of his brothers and peered beyond them to his mother and sister.

Upon seeing them, he had trouble believing what his eyes revealed, as if he needed to awaken from a dream again. He blinked hard twice, and as he realized he was not still asleep, his mouth involuntarily began to open slightly in shock. There, resting in the arms of both his mother and Amiee, were two tiny babies, smaller than any he had seen before. Their eyes were closed, and their chests inhaling and exhaling slightly. B could only see their faces as they were wrapped in what appeared to be pieces of his mother's and Amiee's clothing. Their wraps were wet and colored with what looked like spots of blood around them. Upon realizing B's arrival, all four of his family members looked to him, each of them with a peaceful and understanding smile. B felt the need to ask a multitude of questions, but his mind seemed unable to connect with his voice to actually speak any of them into the early morning air. After a few seconds, Rose looked back down into her arms and spoke softly.

"Good morning, Bikonzi. Let me introduce you to your two newest brothers: Gelor and Andre."

B remained lost for words for at least a minute, able only to stare and take in this incredible revelation. He was not positive precisely what he was to expect, but he certainly failed to anticipate two new brothers when falling asleep the night before. He also wondered why she had named the boys after the two commanders. His mother had always talked about how important names were to her and, more broadly, to their family and people. Why waste the names of such vile people on her sweetest new additions to the family?

"Why Gelor and Andre?" he asked her instinctively.

After a brief pause, Rose replied:

"Those commanders have forgotten who they are. Maybe these twins can remind them."

He processed her words silently, surrounded by his family, who stared wildly at the new creatures. After a few moments, Amiee spoke.

"Do you want to hold him?" she asked B as she looked up.

B was silent for a few seconds, breaking with a near-breathless gasp.

"Sure," he replied.

Amiee slowly and gingerly stepped toward B, all the while keeping the child close to her chest. She leaned toward him, gently releasing the child into B's waiting arms.

"Make sure to support his head as you hold him," she said.

Once she was confident B had a firm grasp, and that Moses and John were supervising him carefully, she stepped away. B's eyes glanced after her, and he now noticed a pile of bloody and wet rags against the wall as well. There was a cord, like a short and shriveled snake, curled near this pile as well, and what appeared to be a piece of bark was sitting adjacent. Amiee collected these items and carried them to the far corner of the room, where no family resided. B's eyes returned to the child.

He stared down and inspected one of his two new brothers for the first time. His eyes were shut tightly. B could feel the slight expanding and contracting of the baby's lungs upon his forearm, and he noticed the sharpness of the shoulder blades as well. Beneath the dirty rags he was wrapped in, he noticed a tight and swollen belly, as if the child had swallowed an entire mango and was digesting it whole. His tiny fingers poked out of his wrap, curled and moving ever so slightly on their own. The baby shifted uncomfortably and grimaced, though no cry accompanied him. He slowly swayed his body back and forth as he and his brothers watched intently.

"Is this Gelor?" he asked his mom without lifting up his eyes.

"No," Rose replied, "that is Andre."

B only nodded in response, beginning to lightly smirk. After a few more seconds, he spoke again.

"How is he going to eat?" he inquired. "He doesn't have any teeth, right?"

"Mom will feed him," John said, jumping into the conversation. "She makes milk for him."

"Milk?" B asked, "Where is she getting milk?"

"Her body makes it," John continued, growing impatient.

"How does that work?" Bikonzi asked, puzzled by John's explanations.

"Just forget about it," John replied. "Let me hold him."

Shifting the conversation, John received Andre and held him tightly against his own chest. Amiee returned with Seth in tow, using each arm and holding them tightly to her body. Bikonzi stepped back slightly and took in the scene again. He saw the collective eyes of his family fixated upon these two new additions, and still, no one spoke as if their arrival had muted the world. As he watched them, he noticed a difference in the light of the room. The clouds outside the place began to split, and a striking and sudden beam of light showed down through the broken window closest to them all. It shone into their midst, and the day had begun.

CHAPTER 12:
CARDBOARD

"Wisdom is like fire. People take it from others."

-African Proverb

Traya had paid close attention to the babies over the coming days. Since her confrontation with John, she rarely initiated interactions with their family, and once the twins were born, she kept her silent eyes often attuned to the family. It seemed that even she, too, was stunned by new life in such a dire space.

News continued quickly throughout the camp following the birth of the twins, making its way out of the room to the guards and their families. Soon, B noticed that work for the boys produced increased wages: John and Moses, in particular, were bringing back nearly twice the amount of food they had before their two newest brothers were born. It seemed as if the very existence of the twins had multiplied the care the family was receiving, and this was echoed one evening shortly following their birth.

After the sun had set and darkness had begun to settle upon them, a woman appeared at the doorway closest to the Moises. She poked her head through at first, glancing slightly around before entering, carrying long, thin strips of cardboard in her hands. Without hesitation, she approached

Rose directly, kneeling just a couple of feet from her. John rose quickly and crouched behind Rose, eying the woman suspiciously. Upon arriving near the family, she spoke two words.

"Thank you."

She set the cardboard down at her side.

Rose did not reply but simply smiled at the woman. It was difficult to tell in the dying light, but it seemed as if her eyes had begun to water. Rose then embraced the woman, hugging her closely for a few seconds. B was confused by this interaction: What was this woman thanking Rose for? Why had she come late at night? What was she doing here?

After releasing their grasp on one another, the woman continued to speak.

"Can I see them?" she asked.

Rose nodded, moving toward the twins sleeping just behind her. As she reached for Andre, she motioned to John and prompted him to pick Gelor up as well. Gingerly grasping the boys, they both shifted back to this woman, who stared and smiled at each of them. Rose lifted Andre to her and, without speaking, offered the woman the opportunity to hold him. She accepted, welcoming the child into her arms and swaying slightly with him. She held and stared at him for a minute or two, and the room was silent. The entire family watched without words as this woman, a stranger to each of them, held their family's newest member, nurturing him as if he were her own. A peaceful stillness filled the air, and for a moment, the family forgot where they were. For a moment, Death had disappeared. For a moment, they had only life.

The woman then abruptly began to speak again, reminded of the cargo she carried with her and her purpose for coming.

"I don't have much time," she said quickly, handing Andre back to Rose. "My husband, Andre, and I just learned of the birth of these two and their names. I had to bring something."

She now grabbed the cardboard that sat behind her and placed it down in front of her.

"It's not much, but it should help a little. You can use them as sleeping mats during the night."

She unfolded five thin strips in front of them, setting them down adjacently and patting each so they lay flat. Motioning to them, she invited Rose to lay down on one of them. Rose looked up, smiled at her in response, and handed Gelor off to Moses so that she could lie down. She eased her body onto one of the pieces, careful not to cause it to slide out from underneath her. Releasing the tension from her arms, holding her up at first, she laid back onto the new, softer surface. Immediately upon setting herself down, she closed her eyes and inhaled a deep breath. A smile came upon her face as she exhaled, and she slowly arose again to hug the woman who had delivered these items.

"Thank you," she said.

After this second embrace, the woman spoke again.

"I must go. Andre would be angry if he knew I was here. I will be sure to send more things your way when I have the chance."

She rose quickly to her feet, and, as abruptly as she had entered the place, she exited. The entire family was in awe. The wife of the commanding officer of the camp had come to care for them! She had held Andre, the namesake of her husband! Bikonzi wondered if this was the reason the guards had ceased their midnight arrivals—perhaps she had some part in this. He glanced quickly over to Traya, who watched from the shadows on the far side of the room and then glanced back to his family.

They all kept their eyes fixed on the doorway for a few seconds in silence, having followed Andre's wife out. Then, as was their nightly ritual, they gathered themselves together, adding and adjusting the pieces of cardboard between them to maximize comfort for each of them. Linked together, they laid down, each able to rest at least a portion of their body on the new cardboard bedding. That evening provided the most restful sleep Bikonzi had felt in months.

The cardboard was only the beginning of the new abundance of resources the family had garnered over the preceding weeks. Food rations continued to increase incrementally until they were nearly triple what they had been. Additional articles of clothing began to arrive for the family, and John had even started to build rapport with a few of the guards, who had begun to see him not simply as a servant but as an asset to them. He did the tasks they did not want or were unwilling to complete and did them without complaining or usurping his place. These changes created a hope in the family that B had not seen since their arrival: meal times arrived with more smiles than before, and their energy levels rose as well. They had found, at least for the last few weeks, a sustainable and increasingly beneficial mode of survival.

In the midst of this shift in tone for the family, Bikonzi noticed an odd trend. Each time that John would leave to work for the guards (nearly daily following the twins' arrival), Traya would leave as well. For three or four days in a row, John would go early in the morning, just as daylight breached the horizon; then, an hour or so later, Traya would leave the room, often returning just an hour or so after she had left. She never brought back food or other resources but instead would quietly re-enter the room, slinking back to her corner as if she wanted no one to know what she was doing. B saw that his mother had noticed this as well and would often stare silently at Traya when she re-entered the room these days. While still ambiguous, it was clear to him that something was not right.

One evening, just two days after this final mysterious trip from Traya, B was awakened from his sleep by a voice. It was quiet and whispering but seemed to come from the window closest to the Moise corner. B did not raise his head to remain unnoticed but opened his eyes slowly to see what might be happening. The voice spoke only one word:

"John," it said.

The words entered the room and evaporated over the heads of the sleeping family. Bikonzi shifted his body slightly, careful not to wake Jay and Seth, who slept just adjacent to him. He wanted to make sure he could see John from where he was.

"John," the voice spoke again, this time with more urgency.

B watched John as closely as he could. His eyes were beginning to adjust to the dark, and he noticed a figure start to stir amidst his family. He could not tell, but it seemed to be John.

"John…" the voice whispered again, with more power than the previous calls.

Following this third instance, B noticed that same figure start to stand, gingerly rising to its feet to remain undetected by the rest of the family and room. As he stood, B could see by the figure's outline that it was John, responding to his name. B could only see his shadowy profile, but the build was obvious to him. He began to step lightly around his family, moving to the door and following the voice. Each step barely made a noise, his feet like the paws of a panther moving along a jungle carpet. B kept his head from turning and following him but listened intently for when John might have left the room. Upon hearing the light shuffling of dirt, he assumed that John's bare feet must have left the place, and B now committed himself to eavesdropping.

Jay had locked herself onto B's left arm, and Seth had sandwiched himself above their heads between them and Rose. B slowly moved his arm, sliding it slightly back and away from Jay. After a few inches of movement, Jay began to roll in the other direction, taking Bikonzi's arm with her. As she did this, B quickly pulled his arm back toward himself, abruptly responding to her movement. This tactic worked: because of his speed and her own movement, he could escape her grasp undetected. He now slowly rose to a crouch and crept to the open doorway. About two feet away from the opening, voices arrived at his ears.

"...to take you," the initial voice spoke, finishing a sentence B was unable to hear from the start. It was a gruff, male voice, what sounded like one of the many nameless guards Bikonzi had heard and seen in passing.

"Why?" John replied, "Don't they see my work?"

"Some of them, yes. But others are suspecting you have other motives."

"Like what?"

"They don't know. But that woman, she has been talking to them."

"Dammit."

Silence followed John's last exclamation. B rested his back against the wall, just adjacent to the doorway. He dared not look out for the risk of being discovered. After a few seconds, the conversation resumed.

"Look, there may be one thing you could do..." the voice broke into the silence.

John did not reply. The voice continued.

"One of the guards that woman has been talking to, he really wants to have Amiee..." the voice left the sentence in the air for John to finish in his mind. Bikonzi wasn't sure what exactly he meant, but it immediately made him suspicious. Why would they want to take Amiee in the first place? And had the guard meant John when he had said, 'to take you'? Why would they want John? His brow turned down in skeptical confusion as he continued to listen.

John again did not reply. The silence continued for a few more seconds.

"It may not work. But you may not have a choice."

After a few more seconds, John spoke again.

"Okay. Thank you."

Suddenly, B heard the shuffling of feet in the dirt moving toward him. Realizing quickly that the conversation had ended, he jumped quickly to return to where he had been sleeping. He took three long strides and, upon arriving next to Jay, fell to the ground as quickly as possible. His heart was racing, and he slammed his eyes shut. The shuffling of the feet stopped, and it seemed John had arrived back at the room. B did not move but strained his ears, and he believed he heard John rest his body back down onto the cold concrete, his head resting upon a corner of his family's cardboard.

CHAPTER 13:
PEANUTS

"Sticks in a bundle are unbreakable."

-African Proverb

The next morning, John, Amiee, and Rose huddled around the twins. B sat up and began to walk to them. They spoke in hushed tones, largely indiscernible. He could make out a couple of words—guards, trade, hope—but before he could piece them together, the three of them noticed his presence and ended their conversation, turning outwards.

"Good morning, B," said Amiee, smiling. She quickly wiped her face, and B noticed her eyes were red and pooled with tears.

"Good morning," he responded.

Though questions flooded his mind, B could not dwell on them for too long as John broke in.

"B, come with me today," he said, motioning with his head to initiate B's movement.

This invitation quickly dissolved his inquiries; the concept of working alongside John would compensate for any confusion he might be feeling. Moses was to join the two of them, but before they left, John approached Amiee directly. He whispered something indiscernible to her and then embraced her, holding a tight hug for ten seconds or so. Upon releasing their grasp on one another, their eyes locked briefly, and then, without speaking, John turned away from her and moved to the doorway. Moses and B followed, again without speaking. As they moved, B glanced back over his shoulder to Amiee, who watched them leave, a few small tears running down her cheeks. Turning back to John, B noticed he had wiped his face with his hand, never averting his gaze. He simply stared, face forward, his eyes locked upon the unknown moments of the future as he strode out of the room.

To this point, neither Moses nor Bikonzi had much experience with the way in which John interacted with the guards other than what little they heard him report upon his return to the room. They had both attempted to avoid the guards as much as possible. While the recent violent interruption of Moses' prayer by one guard had deterred Bikonzi initially from leaving the room, his fear ultimately subsided because of his increasingly comfortable nearness to Death. 'What's the worst they could do to me anyways?' he'd think to himself. 'If they kill me, they free me, and it's one less mouth to feed.'

While these thoughts catalyzed his excursions, he focused his efforts on the wives, who seemed to have more compassion than their husbands. Bikonzi knew that his size alone really prevented him from doing much in the way of productive work, and he had even grown proud of his approach, as he had managed to avoid any real labor in favor of timing his arrivals in line with the compassion he knew he could garner. Today, however, it was clear as they followed John: they would work.

Without hesitation, John walked directly to the barracks rather than the homes of the few select guards who were married. This approach was new and rather intimidating for B: he had intentionally avoided this building as a means to avert the guards there. Yet John's confidence was sufficient for him; it seemed clear he had done this before.

Upon arriving at the door, John was met by one of the guards. He wore a helmet and dirtied white undershirt and smoked a cigarette when he appeared out of the doorway. The matching of their arrival with his appearance was impeccable, and B assumed this must have been planned or at least something done before. John spoke first.

"I've got these two with me today. What do you need for us to do?" John asked.

The guard looked at Moses and B, briefly staring them up and down.

"Okay," he said, "we can use the bigger one."

Bikonzi immediately recognized the guard's voice: it was the voice he had heard the night before, the voice that had spoken with John. He could not dwell on this revelation for too long, though, as John had turned to look at both Moses and B. Scanning them briefly, he nodded and spoke.

"Alright," he said, "B, get out of here. Go back to the room and wait for Moses and me to come back tonight."

Bikonzi loathed this command initially; he didn't want to spend any more time in that room than he had to. However, knowing that he did not want to upset the guard or disrupt the clear relationship John had built with him, he replied affirmatively.

"Okay," he said.

As he turned to walk away, B could hear a few more instructions from the guard, fading as he continued. After about fifty yards of walking along the roadside, he approached one of the homes he had swindled before. He turned back and glanced over his shoulder to see if John and Moses could see him. It appeared that they were still speaking with the guard, and their backs were faced to B. Turning back in front of him, B walked adjacent to the house on his right and, immediately upon passing it, swiftly ducked behind the wall. He sat and crouched, straining his ears to listen for any activity indicating the others had seen him. No footsteps or voices came for a minute or two.

Crouching and hiding, Bikonzi noticed Christian walking up the road only a few dozen feet away, moving in the other direction, and he decided to call out to him.

"Hey. Christian," he spoke.

Christian turned and speedily walked toward B.

"Hey B," he said as he arrived, "What are you doing over here?"

"John had told me to go back to the room, but I don't want to be stuck in there."

"Ah. Me neither. That's why I'm walking around. You should come with me—I've got an idea."

"An idea? What is it?"

"A few days ago, while I was working for one of the wives, I noticed that there are gardens outside those last two houses. They've got a ton of peanuts scattered around, and I think we might be able to take some."

Christian pointed to the houses he was referring to. They were the final two homes on the far end of the road, bracketing the north and south sides where the snaked path ended. They were also the most heavily supervised—at least one guard was present at each, ensuring that no one entered or otherwise infringed upon the space without consent.

"Don't they have guards waiting outside?" Bikonzi responded. He was a bit nervous, particularly given their last misadventure and brush with danger.

"Yes, but they won't do anything," Christian replied. The worst they could do isn't worse than what they've already done."

This reasoning sounded familiar to B. It sounded like his own. What was the point in avoiding danger if everyone was to be killed off anyway? Why not simply do whatever we want? Death's presence seemed to have loosened his grip on life. Christian's words made sense to him, and so he decided to join him.

"Okay," he said, "let's go."

It's not really stealing, B thought to himself as he joined Christian along the dusty road, positioning himself on the opposite side of Christian so that John and Moses would not see him. His feet warmed as the morning sun heated the ground, shining through sparse cloud cover. *They aren't trying to stop us anymore*, he continued. *What they did to us was steal. What they did to my life was stealing. This isn't stealing.*

There was a boldness that characterized their steps as they went. Christian seemed not to care in the least about the potential of getting punished for their actions; despite the occasional eyes of the passing guards upon them as they went, going about their business in the camp, he did not avert his gaze or turn his eyes down. This again inspired B: he didn't feel the need to sneak around when he was with Christian. He mimicked his walk and smiled slightly as he did; this was the best he had felt in weeks.

As they approached the last two houses, they both noticed a guard stalking around each of them. They were both armed and attentive, ensuring no one approached without their knowing. Without saying anything, Christian began to direct his course to the house on the north side of the road. Bikonzi followed suit, speeding up his walking to ensure he stood directly next to Christian.

They were seen from a distance by the guard charged with watching the house.

"Get out of here, cockroaches!" he said sternly, taking calm and steady steps toward them. He held his gun loosely in his hands.

Christian did not slow his walk or respond, instead choosing to close the gap silently. When he had reached about fifty feet, the guard spoke again.

"Are you deaf? I said leave!" the guard stated again.

"We heard you," Christian said, "We just thought you may want some help."

"What would I need *your* help with?" the guard scoffed.

"Small tasks, of course. Maybe some things you don't want to do on your own time…" Christian allowed this to be a leading statement, hoping the guard would fill in the blank.

Instead, he stared mildly at the boys, leaving silence for a few seconds. Then, B noticed a small bag dancing across the dust between them, blown by the wind.

"We could clean up the trash around the house for you," he spoke instinctively.

Both Christian and the guard turned in surprise to the previously silent boy.

"You won't have to worry about any of the trash. We can clean it up for you," he repeated. "You can watch us while we work."

Both boys turned and looked at the guard again, awaiting his response. He was at first annoyed; he didn't seem to want to deal with them at all. Yet the prospect of sitting down in the midst of his shift visibly worked its way across his face, and he began to think. Looking down at first, he seemed to be balancing the proposition in his mind. After a slight, nearly imperceptible nod, he spoke.

"Alright, that's fine. Start cleaning up trash around the house. Just remember, I'm watching you."

Christian turned and smiled slightly at B, and they began.

B had never grasped how much trash the wind would float around the camp until he was forced to clean it up. Cigarette butts, empty plastic bags, half-eaten fruit pieces—with his eyes down, he was able to see the garbage exponentially more than he had. Neither boy had any place to store their trash before disposing of it in the nearby dumpster, so they stretched out the bottom of each of their shirts to carry as much as they could in one trip.

The guard watched them closely at first, ensuring that they were indeed following the terms of the initial agreement. After witnessing a few trips back and forth, he chose to sit and continue his watch, resting in the shade as the sun continued to bear down. The threat of these boys affected him less as their work continued. Before long he began to close his eyes; he snapped himself awake from time to time as his head bobbed downward, but he continued to fade in and out of consciousness. This enabled the boys a bit of time to investigate the area, maintaining their trash pickup but declining in their efficiency as they looked around.

Sure enough, just as Christian had anticipated, a small garden full of peanut plants sat on the north side of the house, just adjacent to the west side where they currently worked. Their eyes both widened, glistening slightly in the sun.

The boys quickly walked back so as to avoid drawing attention. They continued to collect bits of trash, carrying them as before, and this time, Christian noticed that the guard watching them had fallen asleep entirely. He thus spoke quietly to B.

"Did you *see* the peanut garden in the back?" Christian asked excitedly.

B figured he must be asking rhetorically, for they had clearly both seen it. He nodded and widened his eyes, silently matching Christian's emotions.

"We should grab as many as we can before he wakes up. Back at home my mom had a few peanut plants; they're always easy to pick. It's just like pulling weeds."

B again nodded, and the boys quietly snuck around to the north wall of the house, leaving the guard to snooze in the shade.

Without hesitation, both boys began to collect as many peanuts as they could hold. They filled their shirts with them in the same way they had with the trash and wasted no time in consuming them as they went along. Some were easier than others: there were a few scattered pods already on the surface, likely dropped or leftover from whomever had picked before; these were easy to grab, crack open, and consume. After a few trips to and from the start to the end of the garden, they shifted their focus to the plants themselves. They began to individually uproot them, revealing an abundance of peanuts underneath the surface; each green and yellow plant was home to at least a dozen peanuts at a time. They worked together to efficiently break the formerly buried pods open before eating them, though their methods differed: Christian had found a rock nearby and began to smash the outer layer to produce the nut inside, while Bikonzi opted to use his teeth.

Slowly, with each passing peanut, they became less aware of their location. The camp, the room, the guard, the whole thing fell away in their minds; they laughed to themselves and joyfully passed the time together, simply content with the state of this moment. Eventually, they sat down together, continuing to eat.

"See, I told you this was a good idea!" Christian said as he cracked open another nut.

Bikonzi nodded. "These are the best peanuts I've ever eaten."

"I know! I want to save some for those who are back in the room, but I also don't; they chose to miss out—"

Christian was interrupted by a loud, abrupt clang from inside the house and some angry shouts. This startled them both, and they quickly shot up from their seats, soil still clinging to their shorts. Any peanuts that had been uprooted were quickly dropped, and they used their feet to stomp them into the ground and hide them as best they could. Their eyes darted from the ground to the back door, an empty rectangle into a black abyss. A second or two passed in silence. Then, Commander Andre emerged from the home.

His walk was one of violent urgency. He clenched his fists tightly as he moved to them. His eyes were strained and red, a mix of confusion and rage emanating from him. B noticed that he did not wear the hat he had originally seen that first day and noticed for the first time that the man was balding; his hair poked out on either side of his head, but the top and middle remained smooth, reflecting in the sun as he moved outside. B also noticed the gun attached to Andre's left hip.

"What do you think you're doing here?" Andre yelled, his forehead scrunched downward and his eyebrows forming a disconnected 'V.'

Neither boy could answer. Christian's left leg quivered slightly, and his eyes did not move from Andre's face. B felt a strange warmth come over him, trickling down from his waist to his legs; the soil he stood had transformed to concrete, and his feet sealed in.

"I said, 'What are you doing here?'" Andre repeated.

His hand now darted toward his gun. Both boys looked at each other, their eyes filled with the thoughts of family, life, and death. A tear welled up in B's right eye.

Andre now grasped the gun from his pocket and held it loosely in his hand. He looked down as he did, moving the weapon back and forth and admiring it. The sun glinted off the clean, black metal and shined into B's eye briefly. Andre began to whisper indiscernibly under his breath, smirking slightly as he did. He froze, took a deep breath, and then sighed. Then, he quickly raised the gun and took a step toward them.

Just as he did, a guard stepped from around the corner of the house and interrupted the commander.

"I told them to clean up the trash around the house," he spoke quickly, taking in the scene.

It was the guard who employed the boys and fell asleep on his watch. He looked directly at Andre as he spoke, glancing quickly at them and squinting as his eyes re-adjusted to the sun.

Andre stared directly at the guard in confusion, lowering the gun slowly as he did. He glanced back at B and Christian, then back at the guard once more. After a few moments, he holstered his weapon, re-entering the house and shaking his head. The three of them all stood silently, staring into the dark doorway. The guard then looked back at the boys; he did not speak, but his eyes urged them to go.

Without hesitation, B and Christian sprinted away from the garden, following the road back to their room. As they moved farther away, more loud banging rang out from within the house, ringing out in the distance. They did not look at one another or look back until the house was long out of sight, eventually stopping to bend over and catch their breath. Christian fell to the ground, resting his body on his arms. B slowed to a stop, bending over and resting his hands on his knees.

As he did, he noted heavy moisture soaked into his pants. He looked down at his legs and saw that they were mostly soaked, particularly in the front, and he realized what that warm feeling had been. During all of the commotion, and amidst his frozen fear, he had failed to recognize. He had peed on himself, thoroughly soaking his lower body. He glanced at Christian, whose heavy breathing continued. Christian simply looked at B, smiling and chuckling slightly, and then glanced away, ensuring no one had followed them. B began to laugh with him, and they continued on their way back to the room.

Upon his arrival, the water that soaked his shorts had cooled, and they now stuck to his legs slightly as he stepped. Upon walking through the door, the first sound he heard was from Rose. She quietly sat in the corner of the room, back pinned where the two walls met, Gelor in one arm and Andre in the other. She was quietly crying, her head bobbing up and down as she did, and her tears slowly dropping to the ground. B's eyes then scanned over the rest of his family in the room. Seth and Team were sitting adjacent to Rose on her right, their backs resting against the wall. Jay was just nearby, slowly chewing her way through a tomato from the night before. It took a few more seconds for him to realize, but when he did, he felt his heart start to sink into his stomach. His throat immediately felt dry, and he swallowed hard. Amiee was gone.

"Where's Amiee?" Bikonzi asked urgently as he approached Rose.

His mother did not answer immediately, but she responded after a few seconds.

"Two guards came and took her today," she said.

"Why?" Bikonzi inquired.

Rose again paused briefly before responding. She needed a second or two to steady her words.

"It was her or John," she replied.

Bikonzi's gaze slowly transferred from Rose's face to the concrete ground beneath them. Her quiet tears narrated his thoughts and questions, which ran quickly through his mind. Why had they taken Amiee and not John? And why had his mother seemingly chosen to give Amiee up and not John? That seemed particularly confusing and unfair. And then, now that she was gone, what would the guards do with Amiee? Each time they had taken someone from the room, it was the last time that B had seen them. Was this the last time he would see Amiee? He quickly cast this thought aside, not desiring to dwell on it himself. Why would they want to take her in the first place? Why would they want to take John?

As he considered these questions, he glanced around the rest of the room. His family remained huddled together; his younger siblings did not have much of a grasp of what was happening, and thus, they simply sat near Rose, either staring at her or crawling and exploring nearby. B's eyes now moved beyond just his family, and his scan landed him abruptly upon Traya's gaze. She stared directly at B, her eyes piercing and unrelenting, her brow angled down and in. A small smirk had arisen upon her face. It almost felt as if she held his attention by a string as if her eyes controlled his own. It was then he realized that Death had not gone away. The twins had only pushed it out of sight for a moment. It still hovered in the place and had employed new recruits as partners in its work. It was more than just Traya staring back at him. It was Death, too.

After a few seconds, he broke free, immediately scurrying to sit next to Rose and offering to hold Gelor. With Amiee now gone, it became clear then that his mother would need all the help she could get.

Around dusk, John and Moses arrived back in the room. Moses' response to Amiee's absence was more vocal than Bikonzi's: he expressed his confusion and anger and initially even wanted to leave the room to find her and get her back. John, however, remained calm, as if the news was not new to him. He calmed Moses, reminding him of the importance of taking care of their family here and now. This was the only thing that they had any control over. "Besides," John said, "They'd kill you before you got anywhere near Amiee. We can't afford to lose anyone else."

Bikonzi understood both of his brothers' responses, feeling at once a longing for action to bring Amiee back and a sense of duty to his family as he saw it in front of himself now. His mind flashed to the recent moments he had neglected that duty: his stealing Gideon's bag of rice and shoveling it all for himself; his insistence on getting as much food as possible for himself during Moses' prayer; his choice to leave the room in favor of staying and helping Amiee and his mother while they cared for the twins. Maybe, if he had been around, he could have prevented her from being taken. Or maybe he could have gone with her so she wasn't alone. This inner conflict ripped at his heart.

The Moises gathered together to eat what food John and Moses had brought back, staring silently toward the ground as they chewed.

CHAPTER 14:
TRANSFER

"One tree cannot be a forest."

-African Proverb

Something like four months passed after Amiee had been taken. Rose continued to pray for her return, but just as the sun set beyond the dense green jungle each evening, the hope of the family set with it. Bikonzi kept Amiee out of his own mind as much as possible, in the same way he had his father—he chose not to consider what had become of her. It was better he didn't.

Without Amiee, the family seemed sapped of what little meaning they had maintained before. Food rewards for the boys' labor continued, and there were even more cardboard deliveries from the wives, but these did nothing to pacify the despair that had descended upon the Moises. John rarely spoke anymore; upon returning from his work, he would disburse food to the others, take his small portion, and eat in silence, slumped against the cold concrete walls. Rose never smiled, and care for her children seemed especially burdensome without Amiee's heart and hands alongside her. B had tried to help where he could here, sometimes holding or tending to Gelor and Andre as a reprieve, but his strength and size often prevented him from sustaining his grasp on them for very long. The twins cried often, a steady and solemn soundtrack to accompany their days.

Early one morning, surrounded by a dense and cloudy day, the room was abruptly and confusingly awakened. Guards had barged in, barking commands before even opting to wake anyone up. Scattered shouts filled the morning air.

"Wake up!"

B was slow to wake, rubbing his eyes harshly and blinking away the dry and crusty bits left from the night. As he did, he noticed the urgency of Rose and John, who scrambled to grab the youngest siblings so that they wouldn't be stepped on or harmed in the confusion of the morning. Moses stood, holding Jay and Seth's hands and walking them to the doorway.

"Cockroaches!"

B thought he heard Moses mutter to himself, "Finally—it's over," as he passed. This grim sentiment sent a shudder over B—Death seemed to have finally taken his brother over, and as the families begrudgingly stepped forward, Bikonzi found it seeping into his soul as well.

"Let's go—get outside!"

One particular guard did not appreciate Bikonzi's lethargic pace. He kicked B from behind and thrust him to his feet toward the door after Moses. There was a jam of people attempting to exit the same door all at once, causing the procession to slow. The guards ushing the mob out, however, seemed to see no conflict between the number of people they were required to move and the open space of the doorway. They shoved the families from behind, the cold metal of their guns pressed into their necks, causing chills to pop up upon the bodies of those they moved, Bikonzi included.

"Out, out!"

Wherever they were headed, it was clear the journey was to be swift.

Upon emerging through the doorway amidst the dense fog and clouds, they were all grouped separately, according to their own units. They were then directed across the road, halted just adjacent to the holes they had dug on their arrival day. The guards who had forced them out joined a small contingent waiting near the holes, armed and silent. B counted eight of them in total, seemingly awaiting command. An open-bed military truck sat running next to the group on the road, dark exhaust leaking its way into the air along with the smell of gasoline. Rose hugged Gelor and Andre close, her chin buried in her chest and her eyes watering. Cries from her family emanated emptily into the air.

There had been a creeping confusion in Bikonzi's mind as to why it had taken them so long to finally come to a conclusion on what was to be done with these families. While their confusion about identities and language might have given them pause, there nevertheless seemed to be a sort of conflict in them. Why keep them there for this long and use resources to sustain them, if only to kill them off later? He wondered if the cheap labor proved more valuable to them than he knew - perhaps dying slaves were better than dead enemies.

Standing in front of the guards were two men conversing quietly over a sheet of paper. One was unmistakably recognizable to him: it was the guard who had taken Amiee for himself in that terrible exchange a couple of months prior. His gun was strapped behind his back, and his eyes were wide and attentive, a posture of patient listening; he would even glimpse, occasionally, at Rose as he spoke. He spoke with a man that B did not recognize. Short but solidly built, the second man wore a fitted dark gray suit and patterned navy tie. His head was smooth and round, and a dark mustache covered his upper lip and wrapped around the corners of his mouth. He stood steadily, pointing from the paper toward the families in his midst and asking questions of the guard next to him. The guard's posture increased in urgency as they spoke and eventually shifted to a sort of pleading, his eyes glancing back again to the Moise family from time to time.

After a few moments of silence following his pleading, the man in the suit nodded thoughtfully, and the guard saluted him before immediately walking urgently back to the buildings where he and the other guards stayed. The man in the suit now stood alone, quietly, his black shoes settling slightly into the damp mud on the ground. He glanced quickly at his watch after a few minutes, turning around his shoulder, presumably to look at whatever he was waiting for. As he looked over his shoulder, Bikonzi's eyes followed him, and in the distance, he saw two figures moving to them—one man and one woman. As they drew nearer, it was clear they were walking together, and he was not coercing her forward in any way. Bikonzi squinted in an attempt to see better, and–almost in unison—Rose gasped aloud at the precise moment B realized who the guard was walking with. It was Amiee.

As she drew nearer, she sped her walk, eventually into a run. She collapsed down into Rose's waiting arms, tears streaming down both their faces as they embraced. B's eyes began to well with tears as he immediately moved to join the embrace in simultaneity with John and Moses. The family hugged and smiled and cried for a couple of brief moments before a second realization came to Bikonzi. In their embrace, his hand had brushed Amiee's belly, and he felt a small bump he hadn't noticed as she approached them. Confusedly, he leaned back, and sure enough, he noticed a clear slope descending from just below her chest to her waist, much like the bump his mother had before giving birth to the twins. She was pregnant.

Bikonzi's eyes glanced quickly over to the guard who had walked her back, and his eyes were locked upon Amiee with a sort of urgency and compassion he hadn't seen before from any of their other captors. *Was he the father?* Bikonzi wondered. *Was he behind bringing her back to her family?* B turned back to Amiee as his mother whispered quietly between their tears.

"You're here, my girl. You're safe. I love you, and we will love this one."

Rose leaned back and ran her hand along Amiee's belly. They shared a small smile together before the man in the suit cleared his throat as an indication he was about to speak. The family turned their attention toward him.

Taking one last glimpse at the paper he was still holding, the man took a pen from his pocket, added one note to the page, and then folded it neatly, placed the pen and page into his suit pocket, and began speaking.

"Good morning," the man started. His eyes were calm and observant, and he glanced methodically over each of the families before continuing.

"There have been some changes to this camp and what is to be done with you all moving forward," he continued. His voice remained as methodical as his eyes, each word rolling with a rhythm that was at once patient and engaging, causing B to lean in and listen. Most of the soldiers behind the suited man stared angrily, tightening grips on their weapons and squinting slightly.

"We believe that this is the best way forward, both for you all and for our nation as a whole, at this time."

He paused now, glancing again at each family. His face neither smiled nor frowned. His voice and posture were devoid of the exaggerated sentiments which characterized the guards who stood behind him.

"Moise family," the man announced, directing three soldiers to them. Within a few seconds, the guards stood behind the family. The metal of the weapons they wore clicked with each step they took. The family remained on their knees, bound tightly together in knots of arms and legs, avoiding glances back behind them. John and Moses had closed their eyes entirely, their heads tilted to the dirt beneath them. B again glimpsed his mother: she had not yet raised her face from her chin, and she now had her eyes closed, her mouth moving indiscernibly. Tears streamed down her face, and her lips moved in what B could only discern as a prayer.

The man looked over them at the soldiers and nodded promptly. B joined his siblings in closing his eyes and looking down as well. He squeezed his eyes hard and clenched his fists, which rested heavily upon his legs. After a couple of seconds, he felt a light nudge in his back, which caused him to loosen his grip confusedly. Another nudge. He turned around and saw a guard extending his gun toward him.

"Get up. We're moving you to the truck," he said, motioning with his eyes in that direction.

B turned his head to the rest of his family. They all stood slowly, looking around at the others who remained seated and gathered together, glancing at the rest of the soldiers who stood at attention, and finally at the man in the suit, who simply stood with his hands behind his back. He wondered why they, in particular, were the ones being led away.

The Moises moved to the running truck and were funneled into the bed. The tailgate was closed, and one soldier tapped it twice before the truck lurched and rumbled forward. As they drove away, B noticed the man in the suit continued to address the remaining families, pointing at and directing them.

The truck kept moving toward the exit of the camp, eventually passing into the jungle outskirts, bouncing occasionally and splashing into and out of mud puddles along the way. Staring out of the open back, B saw they had passed a group of three women, all carrying baskets upon their heads. They looked back to the truck that passed them, and B recognized them as the wives of the soldiers he had met before. As they quickly sped into the distance, Bikonzi could see that they were smiling. He considered it must have been them, and perhaps some combination of this soldier who brought Amiee back, that prompted their present exit from the camp. He looked quickly at Rose now and saw that she, too, was smiling and staring back. B couldn't help but smile himself.

The truck bumped and bounced its way for about thirty minutes, grazing itself upon a choir of rustling tree branches and, eventually, moving into the dirt roads of Mbuji-Mayi. Houses–some brick, but mostly mud, with thatched roofs matching many of the homes in the camp–were buried amidst dense, green brush as if planted right alongside them. Rain began to fall as they drove, seeping into the bed of the truck as well. As the water fell, B's mind was flooded with questions: who was that man in the suit? Where were they being taken? What did this mean for their family? He glanced at Gelor and Andre, who rested in the arms of Rose and John; what was to happen to them? And what about Amiee? The more distance put between her and them meant the more questions—and doubt—about her safety and reunification with the family. B knew he was glad to be far from the smells and sights of that camp, but he wondered whether knowing was better than not knowing.

Amidst these thoughts, he began to notice another truck in the distance. It was small at first, its dark green metal and canvas overhang blending in amidst the trees and hidden amongst the falling drops of water. As they drove, it grew bigger in B's vision, approaching them rapidly. As it did, he heard the shouts of the drivers of his own truck. Though their words were indiscernible, they were urgent in their tone, and they quickly accelerated their pace. Rose and John watched as well, grasping Gelor and Andre in their hands tightly as the truck jostled back and forth.

"Someone didn't want us to leave," Rose said aloud.

Another change in driving surface: from dirt roads, they moved onto a smooth, paved road and began to speed up rapidly. As they accelerated, B noticed the backs of signs and the cars they passed as they went. The truck lurched right and left, weaving its way through traffic and prompting the honks of frustrated drivers. Wherever they were headed, they were in a hurry.

The truck that followed them matched their every move, continuing to close the gap. As they did, B noticed that there was a soldier beginning to lean out the passenger window. He held tightly onto the inside of the truck with his left hand, and as he extended his right hand out the window, B noticed a machine gun aimed in their direction. Upon seeing this, the family all quickly turned their backs and huddled as low together. Gunshots rang out through the morning, and more honking from the cars around them added to the chaos. Bullets ricocheted, banging against the metal of the truck like a flurry of rocks thrown upon a tin roof. B opened one eye from beneath his shielded head; Rose was glancing around to see if anyone had been hit, and upon realizing no one had, she quickly returned back to her ducked position. It seemed they were in the clear.

Then, as abruptly as they had changed to this smoother roadway, the Moises' truck now exited. They shot through a gap in the surrounding traffic and sped away, and as they did the truck that had been trailing them was unable to reach the same exit in time, speeding by as the Moise family disappeared into the surrounding neighborhood. In the brief moment of the chasing truck's passing, B noticed two soldiers halfway hanging out its open back, holding tightly onto a pole and staring angrily toward them. They sped off along the freeway, disappearing out of sight amidst the rest of the traffic.

The Moise's truck continued forward for a couple of minutes, and then a sharp left turn tossed the family in the bed. Only a few moments later, they jerked to a stop. The engine quit its rumbling, and rapid footsteps crunched the dirt next to them. The bed was then opened, and one of the soldiers hurriedly waved them out.

"Let's go! We need to go!" he yelled.

They rushed out into a wide, flat space. To the north, a long and broad asphalt pathway stretched as far as B could see, running right up against a group of large green trees and the backs of a few homes to the south. Just a few feet away, he noticed a thin white airplane, only big enough to fit maybe twelve people. It was parked facing the long strip in front of them.

Then, as if a giant creature emerging from the jungle, a colossal gray plane came into sight, slowly rolling along the asphalt. A loud, steady whine emanated from the beast, provoking the already disturbed children to burst out into loud cries. The soldiers tried to push the family into a jog onto the runway toward the plane, scooping up the little ones in the process so that they could all move forward together. The elder Moises followed this example, running to the plane amidst the soldiers' protection. As they ran, B noticed the back portion of the plane begin to slowly open, a heaping metal ramp descending from the roof. The whine of the engines became deafening as they moved closer, drowning out even the loudest cries of the children.

The ramp hit the ground just as they came to it, and one of the soldiers yelled to the family, barely audible to them.

"You need to get on this plane! You've been transferred."

John nodded and moved the family together up the ramp and into the body of the plane. The rain had picked up now, pelting the metal all around them. B followed Rose in the front, passing stacks of wooden boxes, guns, and ammunition along the way. He glanced behind himself as he stepped. John was ensuring each of the family members was able to get onto the ramp and, upon accounting for them, turned and nodded to the soldiers who waited at the door. The ramp began to rise to the roof again, and the plane began to roll itself forward as it did. B stared out the back of the slowly ascending metal ramp, and as he did, he noticed a military truck emerge from the trees adjacent to the runway and burst onto the asphalt a few hundred feet away. It seemed their pursuant had not given up.

They were attempting to speed toward them again, but as they did, the plane picked up its pace as well. The engines grew louder, the whining and rain now entirely deafening, starting now to overwhelm the whines of the littlest ones. The family huddled together, and B noticed Rose's mouth moving again. He could not hear any words, but with her eyes slammed shut, it seemed she was praying. Then, after a few seconds, they felt the plane lift from the ground. B's stomach was jolted down to his feet, and his back was pinned against the metal wall behind him. As they rose, they heard a few scattered knocks against the back of the plane, akin to those they had heard in the truck on the freeway. Then, only the sound of the plane and the rain remained, accompanying their incline. It was only then that B could fully realize what had happened. They may not have known where they were going, but he knew now: they had made it out.

CHAPTER 15:
PURGATORY

"If love is a sickness, patience is the remedy."

-African Proverb

The flight was loud and bouncy for most of its duration. To avoid falling and rolling around the metal bay, B braced his hands behind his back and on either side of himself much of the time; with no seats to ride in, his mind and body were focused on staying put on the plane. Glancing around, B squinted to notice the abundance of military equipment surrounding them. Beyond this, the windowless behemoth made it impossible for him to see much, with only a few slowly blinking red lights scattered symmetrically across the bay, providing clarity.

Despite the cold and dark metal encasement, Bikonzi could glimpse Rose and John a few feet away, sitting slouched against the side of the plane, arms lying limply at their sides and eyes closed. Their breathing was methodical and deep, as if they were savoring each inhale. It reminded him of when he would hold his breath for as long as he could after going underwater: eventually, upon bursting to the surface, the air that filled his body tasted different. It looked like Rose and John were breaking the surface for the first time in months.

It did not take long for them to begin their descent. B noticed it first when Seth and Illunga began to slip toward the front of the plane along the metal, unable to hold themselves. He quickly caught the former, and Moses helped with the latter, as Rose and John had their hands full with the twins. Upon both catches, B glanced at Moses, and they began to chuckle with each other. They held their brothers as the plane continued. After a few more minutes, short screeches sounded around them, alarming B at first. He looked to Rose immediately, who met his concern with a small smile.

"We're just landing," she said.

As the plane slowed, the noise of the engines dwindled, replaced by more raindrops pelting the outside. Finally, they came to a halt, and the back ramp descended. B expected people to be waiting outside the plane as it did, but they were met only by wet asphalt and steady rain. No one directed them, and after a minute, John led the family out.

Upon reaching the tarmac, B noticed the largeness of this airport compared to the last. Squinting through the water as it streamed down his face, he saw a long, flat horizon with scattered trees blowing in the wind. They waited briefly outside the plane, expecting someone to emerge after them and direct them where they needed to go. Instead, it sat there unmoving, and after a minute or so, the ramp rose again, closing off the back of the beast. It rolled itself back off to the runway, preparing to leave the airport just as quickly as it had arrived. They were on their own, it seemed, and B—mirroring Rose and John—began to survey the landscape more thoroughly.

There was a large, yellow-orange tower looming about a hundred yards away. It stood adjacent to a glass-windowed building, other planes of various sizes lined nearby. They speedily walked toward this tower and building—soaked, exhausted, and confused. Upon reaching them, they noticed lights shining through from inside the glass building, radiant through the light fog that hung in the air. John continued to lead them there and, upon arrival, noted a door they could enter through. Without hesitation, he opened it and led the family into the place.

The first thing Bikonzi felt was the rush of cool air upon his face and body. It immediately brought chills to his skin, and he grabbed his arms in an attempt to warm them. As he did, he began to look around, but he was overcome by the mass of people around him. Men in shirts and ties and women in bright purple, yellow, and pink scurried throughout the building, indifferent to this family and preoccupied with unseen business. To see people clothed, fed, and living normally was utterly disorienting to him. In their time in the camp, it seemed that time had paused and that the whole world had been condensed down to those buildings and that road and their suffering. And now it was as if the world in which he had lived the last few months was a grim fantasy, an unreality, to the world which continued hurriedly along in front of him now, indifferent to him and his family.

A few rows of chairs were unused to their left, and John shuffled the family to sit. No one spoke amidst them but simply followed John's lead, unsure of what would come next. They arrived at the empty chairs and sat in and around them. They watched, remaining silent, for a few minutes; B noticed John's eyes were wide and scanning the place. He seemed suspicious, on edge. Then, eventually, they were approached by a man dressed in a blue uniform, donning a black hat and other regalia. As he approached, he looked them up and down. His eyes showed confusion as he did, attempting to make sense of this group before him. Eventually, he spoke.

"Hi there. Can I help you?" he asked.

Rose took the initiative to respond.

"We were just dropped onto the tarmac by a cargo plane," she explained.

The man's confusion increased, evident by his cocked head and squint.

"Where are you coming from? And where are you headed?"

Silence for a few moments.

"We don't really know."

The man continued to look confused. B could tell he was thinking hard about what to do.

"Well, do you have any tickets?" he asked.

"No."

Again, confusion and thinking.

"What's your name?" he continued.

"Rose Mapendo—Moise," Rose replied.

This was the first time Bikonzi had heard his mother say her name in over a year. It was almost foreign to him. She included her maiden name before tacking on her married name here, and for the first time since they had been taken, he had considered his mother's namesake. He recalled that Mapendo, in Swahili, meant love.

"Got it," he replied, scribbling her name on a small sheet of paper he pulled from his pocket. Let me see what I can do." He walked away, turning his head in a couple of different directions as if looking around for where he might need to go next. Eventually, he disappeared into the sea of travelers, all rushing to their own business.

B continued to scan the place. The chairs rested their backs against a large, white wall, which spanned thirty feet, starting from the glass windows of the building and moving to the inward parts of the airport. There was a sort of walkway at the end of the wall, where most of the foot traffic went back and forth, either disappearing beyond it or continuing in the other direction. There was another wall about 100 feet in front of them, the same length and directed the same way, stretching toward the walkway as well. They were in some kind of side section of the place, kept away from the highest amount of activity. B noticed a drinking fountain connected to the wall in front of him and immediately, involuntarily, sprung to his feet and walked to it.

Seeing what he had noticed, John and Moses joined, and soon, all three of them were jockeying for position around the device. They each tossed elbows into each other's stomachs, pushing until they had eventually decided on an order; John drank first, with Moses following and Bikonzi finishing their rotation. Then, they took turns shuffling the other, smaller children over to the fountain to drink. Rose was the last to sip from the fountain and stood there for a few minutes. They returned to their chairs again, simply waiting for the man to return.

He didn't for a long while. Hours passed, and the Moises fell in and out of sleep together, some strewn across the carpeted floor and others in their chairs. In the midst of their scattered resting, questions arose in Bikonzi's mind again. While this was certainly better than the camp conditions, why were they at the airport in the first place? Who had brought them? And if they had a plan beyond here, why were they still waiting? It was as if everything, the whole movement of the world around them, was just unconcerned with them.

The sun started to set that evening, and the room swapped the more natural, gray light of the day with the yellow, faded indoor light instead. Finally, the man returned. B noticed that he carried a disappointed look as he approached them.

"I'm so sorry for the delay, Rose. I work for one of the airlines here, and I spent the last few hours trying to track down your name, or any record of your having flown here," he paused briefly, then continued.

"I found nothing. I'm not sure how you all got here, but unless you have tickets, there isn't a lot we can do. I'm sorry."

Rose's response was quiet but seemingly unsurprised. She nodded back to the man, acknowledging him and allowing his news to sink into her mind. Her nod and thinking silence seemed to spark a deeper desire to help in the man; he took a deep breath and spoke again.

"There might be one more thing I can do," he said, "Let me speak with my manager—I'll be right back."

Rose again nodded, responding, "Thank you," to the man's kindness.

He nodded in reply and walked away.

Rose sat back, wordless in her chair, and closed her eyes.

Another day passed as the family waited. Without food, they moved little, opting to remain in their small corridor. There was a public toilet around the corner that they utilized, and they continued to drink from the drinking fountain in large quantities. B noticed, from time to time, distracted faces of passerby's glance in their direction. Some of them shot confused looks their way, others grimaced in response to their smell, but all of them continued without stopping. It was only after these two days, early on the morning of their third day, that they were finally approached again. This time, the man who had helped them led two other men with him; the other two men wore suits, one brown and one blue. B's eyes were drawn instantly to their shoes, which shone brightly, reflecting the yellow lights above their heads.

The man they already knew stopped a few feet short of them, then stepped just to his right and out of the way of the men in suits, who surveyed the family before them briefly. Then, they glanced briefly at each other before looking back at the Moises and uttering two words.

"Get up."

John was the first to stand without any resistance. He scooped up Andre, and Rose, Moses, and John followed his lead. Seconds later, they were following these men through the middle of the airport amidst the sea of other travelers. The looks increased exponentially now, as others held more prolonged stares as they passed. Eventually, the family was shown through a brown door, which led outside to a stairwell. It wound down along the side of the airport building to the tarmac, where they were again ushered onto another cargo plane, quite similar to the last one. The men in suits ensured the family boarded the plane, and soon, they found themselves ascending into the air, headed somewhere they did not yet know.

This flight was far more turbulent than the last, and given the experiences of the last few months, nervousness was all that Bikonzi could feel. Any time they had been transferred onto a vehicle or moved from one place to another by men he didn't know, it only led to what felt like a disaster. He could only anticipate the same here. Whether due to this nervousness or the bouncing ascent of the plane, B felt nauseous as soon as they got off the ground. It took only 15 minutes in the air for him to vomit. Given the little food in his system, it was largely liquid and clear.

His younger siblings soon followed suit, and the smell worsened over the proceeding hours. This made it quite difficult to rest, and so B rode the rest of the way with a churning and bubbling stomach, in pain from the lack of food.

A few hours later, this second flight landed, and again, the back ramp descended onto a runway. This time, the runway was largely made of dirt and clay, flattened to allow for planes to land more smoothly. The runway was located amid a giant clearing of jungle; as they stepped out into the cloudy day, walls of dark green trees surrounded them on all sides. Gazing around, B only noticed two small, tan structures that stood prominently a few hundred feet away. A woman approached them from the direction of these structures and greeted them near the plane.

She attempted to make herself heard over the sound of the airplane, but her yells fell short of the ears of any of the Moise family. Waving her hand and beginning to walk back to the buildings, the Moises followed suit. Glancing at his older brothers as they walked, B noticed suspicion on the faces of John and Moses. Their eyes were darting around the area, showing little trust in this new situation. While his stomach still turned in pain, B mimicked his brothers' posture: he knew not what he might contribute, but he hoped to contribute, nonetheless.

As they neared the building, one thing in particular struck Bikonzi: the facility had doors. After their time in the doorless, windowless warehouse, this new place had doors, which was particularly noteworthy. The woman, still without a name to the Moises, stepped to the door, grabbed the handle, and spoke for the first time since her attempts to speak over the plane.

"Come in," she said through a small smile and kind eyes.

The door opened up into a small, square room. It, too, had concrete floors, but unlike those in the warehouse, this floor was smooth and unbroken. B's scarred feet welcomed a consistent surface. Two other families were in the room already, and each of them stared at the Moises as they entered. John remained cautious as they did, his eyes bouncing back and forth between each of the other families in the room.

"Please, take a seat and rest here. We'll get you some food and water," the woman chimed in. She walked toward another door, shutting it behind her and disappearing to some other part of the building.

The Moises huddled themselves into a corner. Rose grasped both Gelor and Andre tightly, sinking down to the floor in exhaustion. The youngest children clung tightly to her while John and Moses formed a sort of perimeter, maintaining their observance of the other families therein. Having the option to move in either direction, B chose to sit and watch alongside his brothers. Sweat began to bead down their foreheads: there was little airflow, and the room was warm and sticky.

A few minutes later, the woman reentered with her hands full. She carried two bowls filled with bread, tomatoes, rice, and beans. She handed one to Moses and the other to B, and the warmth of the food emanated from the bottom of the bowl to his hands.

"It's not much, but it's a bit of something. I'll see if we have some clothes for you as well," she said.

He looked down into the bowl and then glanced over to the rest of the family. Moses was already distributing the food to Rose and his younger siblings from his own bowl. Their eyes, though still red and tired, had changed. They were no longer glazed over; they widened and focused, enlivened by this food. B began to distribute the contents of his bowl to the rest of the family as well, and the food was gone in just a few short minutes. Self-preservation had been his default position for so many months, particularly when food was involved, but something had changed in him here. Freedom from the confines of the camp had produced a feeling of freedom to see things with less scarcity, even if only in this small example.

Upon eating them, Rose told the boys to come near to her and the rest of the little ones.

"This," she said, "is the work of God. We must pray and praise what God has done for us here!"

She sat back against the wall and lightly sang, encouraging the boys to sing with her.

"Wahamba nathi, oh," she began.

The tune and lyrics immediately flashed Bikonzi back to Sunday mornings when they were back at home, before all of this. He remembered his mother, standing and swaying and moving their arms alongside a dozen other women in their church.

"Wahamba nathi, siyabonga," she continued, closing her eyes and slowly swaying to the tune.

B joined in at this point. As he did, he closed his eyes, and the picture of the room changed around him. He was no longer here, sitting on concrete amidst a group of strangers; he was in the midst of a church service with his family. He saw men and women dancing and swaying; he saw his father looking smilingly down at a guitar he picked and strummed; he saw his grandfather leading others from the front, clapping his hands alongside the tune. For as much as he had been frustrated with his mother's stubbornly resistant faith, he felt it, in this moment, to be a quenching to his heart, as much as the food quenched his hunger.

"Leha nka tsamaya kgohlong ya moriti wa lefu," Rose sang.

With his eyes still closed, B heard John and Moses quietly join.

"Jesu hobane o na le nna," Rose kept going.

Their singing continued for the next few minutes, and B felt his chest begin to soften and his mind begin to ease. Soon, Rose's singing turned into humming and then into silence. He sat in this silence for a bit, allowing himself to be transported back home.

When he opened his eyes again, he saw two worlds. One was in the face of Rose. With her eyes still closed and her body gently rocking, he saw a world of peace, of hope, of life. This was the world he longed for, the world he wanted to return to. But there was another world he saw. It was in the rest of the room. The faces, of fear, of exhaustion, of pain. It was the room of Death, that same Death that he had known now for so long. And no effort to shut his eyes, no longing gaze into the face of his mother, could rid him of either world. Hope endured, and Death remained, both as near to him as the sweat on his brow.

Later that evening, the woman arrived with new clothes and even sandals for all the Moises and the rest of these families. While not noteworthy in themselves, they were greatly welcomed by B and the rest of his family. Peeling off their clothes at this point meant peeling off the stench and memories of the last few months, and even the thinnest sandals could help heal the calloused and bruised feet that had carried them through the recent days.

However, a tension of receptivity and suspicion remained present over the following two days, if only out of habit from their time in the camp. Food continued at regular intervals, but given the similarity of this room to the previous room where they had been imprisoned, John remained particularly cautious. He slept little and, during the day, ensured his eyes could see the entirety of the room, including the entrances and exits.

While B remained excited that he didn't need to work for food here, he chose to adopt his brother's cynicism. After all, not much had truly changed: they still felt trapped in a building far from home, and it was unclear whether remaining here or attempting to escape was a more dangerous option. The lack of familiarity with the families, space, and future produced a quiet acknowledgment amongst them—words were rarely shared, but knowing glances and trust had developed silently amongst themselves. Rose's songs and prayers would continue, and while B participated in them, such positivity actually pushed him deeper into his own despair with the situation. He loved his mother, but her disposition seemed far too cheery for him, given the lack of clarity on what might be next.

On the third day, when the light had just started to peek through the clouds and leak into the glass-paned windows of the room, there was noise just outside the main door the Moises had been led through by the woman upon their arrival. The gurgling of an engine and crunching of rock and clay indicated some vehicle was approaching. A piercing screech indicated the car had come to a stop, and the smaller crunching of boots upon the earth escalated slightly. In hearing this, John shifted his body so that he could stand between the main door and his family, his eyes fixed on who or what might enter through the door and his legs primed to move at any moment. Moses squatted closely behind his right shoulder, and B stepped into the same position on his left. As the boots drew louder, they suddenly ceased, replaced by the muttering of muffled male voices. This was not the woman who had brought them here and who had kept providing them food along the way. The talking ceased and it was silent for a few moments. The boys braced themselves. That was when the door was opened.

John's head jumped only slightly, the breaking of the silence surprising even his expectant posture. Two men entered, both stout and authoritative. It only took a few moments for concern to arise on the faces of the entire Moise family. John readied himself defensively upon his recognition, his face coiled in anger and distrust. It was obvious to Bikonzi why he had such a reaction, for they knew these men. The first that they recognized was unmistakable: it was the guard who had taken Amiee away from them in the camp. He wore the same uniform, stained with sweat in the armpits, which were visible as he moved his hands and spoke to his companion. The second man was the one who had spoken with the families on their final day in the place and who, it seemed, was responsible for their transfer. He stood slightly taller than the guard and donned a dark blue suit wrapped around a white shirt and blue tie, with the same dark mustache and shiny-shaven head glistening with beads of sweat.

Their attention scanned the room while they conversed quietly. B could tell they spoke in Swahili but could not pronounce their specific words. There was an urgency in the voice and expression of the guard, and every few seconds, he would point directly to the Moises. The bald man listened quietly and responded calmly during the entire conversation, and after each response, the guard seemed increasingly exasperated. Eventually, they both became silent, the bald man looking around the room and the guard now looking down at his feet. Into this silence, the bald man spoke in the same low and commanding voice they had heard before.

"You will come with us," he said matter-of-factly, speaking Lingala. He motioned to every family in the room.

The bald man then stepped back outside, and each family paused briefly. Bikonzi felt what they all manifested in this pause: a lack of trust. Whatever these others had been through, it had clearly mirrored some of their experience, particularly with men in uniforms like this.

The guard noticed their pause and softened his body posture with a slight nod of acknowledgment. Without words, he prompted their movement with an inviting and urgent wave of his hand. His eyes met the group's in an expression that Bikonzi could only understand as compassion. It reminded him of the way some of the wives in the camp had looked at him and his siblings over the last few years. Whatever animated their hearts and eyes, this man had it too.

This look and gesture de-paralyzed the families, who began to proceed out through the narrow door; they were ushered to a large, open-bed truck lined with wooden slats on each side and a large metal chain running along the backside. There were two other guards there to help with the process, ushering the families into the back of the truck and undoing the chain to allow them to pile in. Upon their arrival, these families now realized they weren't the only ones being taken along this next journey: there were dozens of others just like them already piled into the back of the truck, so much so that there hardly seemed to be enough room for these new additions.

John was the last one to leave the room, ensuring that every member of his family had left. B decided to hang back with John, as did Moses; the rest of the families joined a tangled web of bodies and a flurry of short cries and motherly coos at the littlest ones. After everyone outside of these three had filled up the space, it became clear that there were few places to adequately sit for the three remaining Moise boys, so upon entering the bed of the truck, they carefully stepped in the midst of the sea of legs and could stand above the rest of the families therein. They each stood near to the wooden beams on the side of the bed, grabbing the beams for support.

Once they had established their position in the back, one of the guards reconnected the chain and tapped the side of the truck twice to indicate to the driver that they could begin their drive. As they rolled to their next unknown destination, B wondered about the bald man. He had only seen him twice, yet this man seemed to have more power than even the most vicious of the guards he had come across each time. What sort of authority did this man have?

"Who was the bald man?" he asked Rose after a few moments of thinking, holding tightly onto the side of the truck as it bumped and bounced forward.

At first Rose ignored the question, probably thinking it may just fade from Bikonzi's mind. Yet, without a response, B asked the same question again.

Rose looked at him squarely in her response.

"That is the president of our country," she said.

She briefly held eye contact with him as if to adequately land the significance of his presence in their midst. B's eyes widened when he heard this news, and he slowly turned away, filled with thoughts. He did not exactly know what a president did, yet he felt the weight of the interaction even more than he had at the moment. Whatever this man had ordered, it was to be final. And wherever they were headed, it seemed clear to him now: it would be definitive.

CHAPTER 16:
THE CROSS

"Truth should be in love and love in truth."

-African Proverb

The trip lasted far longer than the legs of John, Moses, and B could stand. The boys had to maneuver themselves after a few hours, finding a way to sit or lay beneath or adjacent to their siblings and attempt some sleep. Upon shifting their positions, B found himself overwhelmed by the tight mass of people. The humid air and constant exhaling of these families left him hot and sweating. It was hard to tell how many people were piled into the back of the truck: he was surrounded by a maze of arms and legs, children and mothers, some naked and some clothed, all exhausted and solemn. He heard few words spoken by anyone along the way, largely scattered smatterings of tears and groans. The sun set and rose once during their ride, and besides some short stops for fuel, their transport kept moving. During the heat of the day, they came upon their next destination. The truck began to slow, and a flurry of voices and activity began to rise above the sound of the engine and exhaust, prompting B to stand again and glimpse through the wooden slats to his side.

As the truck bounced forward through hardened mud, B took in the scene through his three-inch-wide gap in the side of the truck. The truck passed under a large banner, upheld by two thin wooden poles staked into the ground; it was faded white and displayed a red cross in its middle. B was overwhelmed by what came next. For as far as he could see, spanning in every direction and all the way to the horizon, a field of white tents came into view. The road they drove on wrapped around these tents and angled to a large metal ramada, under which stood a large crowd. As they drove, B noticed the bustle of activity: he saw mothers corralling and calling and disciplining their children; he saw an abundance of bright outfits and headdresses; and, most notably, he saw—for the first time since they had been taken from their home–men who were not armed and dressed in military garb.

While the tents were all uniform, appearing the same size and color to B, the people who walked through and around them seemed of all different states. Some appeared quite wealthy: their clothes were relatively clean, and their eyes lacked the woundedness that had become customary to B over the last year. Others seemed far nearer to the condition of every person in the truck: the little clothing they wore was dirtied or tattered, implying to B either a difficult journey to this place or extended time in these white tents. As they drew closer to the large ramada, more voices came into view. He could hear different languages–Lingala and Swahili among them, but also languages he didn't know—hectically spoken amidst the large group. While much of the land looked like home, the air and the people felt foreign to him. As the truck came to a stop adjacent to the large ramada, one voice rang out loudly above the rest, amplified by some sort of microphone or megaphone.

"There is food enough for everyone!" the voice spoke with authority and urgency. This statement was reiterated in multiple languages before the voice moved on to its next words.

"Please be sure you have the bowl and spoon given to you when you arrived."

A woman suddenly appeared around the back end of the truck, accompanied by two men donning red vests. Her eyes scanned the mass of families, then briefly spoke to the two men before undoing the chain on the end of the truck. Once she did, she motioned with her hand for the families to move to her, a small and kind smile arising upon her face. She helped in grabbing the smallest children and letting them down off the truck, while the two men with her assisted in helping the women and larger children. John was the first off the truck, promptly turning and helping the older men; meanwhile, Rose quickly left the bed of the truck and urgently drew her children to her. From what B could tell, each of the other older women did the same, and soon the bed of the truck was empty and each of the families had gathered into themselves. The crowd of voices continued as background noise amidst these efforts at the organization, and the same amplified voice rang out above them, repeating the same sentiments to the mass of people.

The woman who had helped them off the truck stepped forward briefly to speak to the driver through the window, and upon the conclusion of their conversation, the truck slowly continued down the road, creating space eventually to turn around and pass them again on its way out of the camp. As the truck did this, the woman now turned her attention to these families. Shouting, she began:

"Welcome!" she said, repeating in numerous languages as well.

"This is the Red Cross at Cameroon. We are here to help you, to get you back on your feet. Each of you will be assigned a tent that you can stay in, and you'll be provided cups, bowls, and spoons for your meals." Again, in each language.

She spoke clearly and directly, yet her eyes and posture maintained compassion as she did. She reminded B of some of the wives he had met at the initial camp.

"There is a grass field just at the end of this road where your children can play. You will be safe here. Follow me to get your utensils and your tent assignment."

She waved to herself and then walked them around the crowd, still clamoring for food, to the other side of the large ramada. As they followed, Bikonzi's eyes were drawn to the foreign faces that fluttered around and by him, again indifferent to him or their presence. It called his mind back to the camp once more, and he wondered what had happened to the rest of the families there. Traya, his cousins, Gideon, Daniel, Amiee—all their faces flooded through his head, a mental crowd to match the physical one that surrounded him. There were long tables set out, upon which were individually organized plastic sets of cups, bowls, and spoons. They were handed out, and each person in the group promptly joined the crowd, pressing in on the source of food.

B quickly found himself lost in the mass. Voices shouted around him and bodies bumped him back and forth. The Moises remained close to one another, with John leading the way. Rose and Moses held the two smallest ones tight, and they moved their way through the ocean of people, bowls and spoons in hand. B kept his eyes on John, who could see over some of the taller people in the crowd and direct the family as they worked their way the food. After a few minutes, a few more long tables came into sight. B noticed two massive silver pots, nearly as tall as him, sitting on a table. One man and one woman had ladles and were scooping some sort of mushy, mysterious food into bowl after bowl, and another man and woman worked behind them over fires, cooking more food in two more silver pots. Eventually, they worked their way to the tables and shuffled themselves through the scooping line.

B wasted no time in beginning to eat. Before they had even found their way out of the crowds and out from under the ramada, he had nearly finished his bowl, so focused upon each bite that he had to be grabbed by Moses to keep moving in the right direction. Upon exiting the ramada, the woman who first greeted them found them again. She led them to another small shade covering, where another man in a red vest sat looking over a paper packet. She spoke directly with Rose, asking where they had come from and how many were in their family, and then relayed the information to the man. He scanned his sheet, flipping through numerous pages, before finally marking something, responding to the woman, and pointing to the valley of white tents B had noticed upon their arrival. The woman nodded, thanked the man, and then prompted the Moises to follow her to the tents.

While they were now away from the crowd's busyness, the flurry of activity persisted. Toddlers scampered around, often followed closely by older siblings or mothers. Clothes were dunked into plastic buckets of water, and numerous laundry lines hung from tent to tent. Small plastic cups and bowls were scattered on the ground, some caked with food residue or mud. Numerous languages were tossed back and forth, creating an ocean of sound that B could only understand a few scattered, individual words.

After a few minutes of winding through these tents, ducking under laundry lines, and avoiding all too deep mud, the woman finally stopped outside a tent whose entry flaps were closed and seemingly untouched. She turned back to the Moises and spoke.

"While you're here, this will be where you can stay. It won't be much, but a couple of cots and blankets are inside. Three meals a day will be served under the ramada–where we just were. Only a couple hundred yards that way," she pointed to her right. "Is the large field I mentioned before. The kids are welcome to play there…"

The woman continued talking, but B's mind had already trailed off to the field. Over the last few months, the only times he had run were for fear of punishment or his life - the notion of running for fun made his chest expand in excitement. He glanced at Moses, who seemed to be having the same simultaneous revelation: he stood on his toes, straining for a glance in the direction the woman had pointed.

By the time B turned his attention back to the woman, she had just finished speaking.

"And that tent there," she pointed opposite the field, "is where you can speak with some of our Red Cross representatives about your status." There was a trailer with a large red cross stamped on the side and a long line of people streaming like ants from its single door.

Rose nodded and gratefully responded to the woman, who walked hastily back to the food ramada, presumably to collect another family and direct them accordingly. They stepped into their tent, a square covering about 15 feet in either direction. Rose sat, holding Andre, on one of the cots the woman had mentioned, letting out a long sigh as she did. B noticed her eyes start to water, and she turned to B directly and smiled. As if she knew what he was thinking, she simply stated to him, "Go play."

B and Moses glanced quickly at each other, smiling, and hurried out of the tent toward the field.

They raced through the lanes between the white tents, their bare feet grabbing and sinking slightly into the moist and muddy ground. B couldn't wipe the smile from his face and he ran, pivoting between glancing over his shoulder at Moses and keeping his eyes forward. He had gotten a head start, but after a few seconds of running, Moses passed him, laughing as he did.

"I'll beat you there!" he said as he brushed B's shoulder and advanced a few steps ahead.

And suddenly, the moment seemed out of time. It flashed his mind back to playing soccer with Moses and his cousins in Mbuji-Mayi: they'd sprint to the haphazardly half-green, half-brown field, bracketed on either end with simple rectangular goals. Often, the game had already begun, and they simply split themselves onto either team to join; for hours, they'd run around that field, kicking and pushing and cheering and yelling. It was as if the breeze on his face now was blowing away the last few months, blowing him back home.

As they neared the end of this mass of tents, the ground elevated slightly, angling upwards to a sort of dirt plateau. Moses arrived first, keeling his body over and resting his hands on his knees as he caught his breath. B arrived immediately after, his own lungs gasping at the same pace as his brother's. B looked out from the top of this small hill, and his eyes landed upon the field only about sixty meters in front of them. Smatterings of wild grass rose above the predominantly brown dirt field. Green metal bars, duct-taped together at the corners, made up the goals, and a group of what looked like twenty kids filled the space. Their voices were at once urgent and joyful, the ball guiding them back and forth across the pitch.

"I'm gonna beat you to the field!" B exclaimed to Moses as he sprinted to join the game. His head start gave him just enough of an advantage, and the boys wasted no time in joining. The game didn't stop for them, so they each chose a direction to go and sorted their teammates from there. The dirt was drier and thinner here, more trampled upon as it was, and there was a thin cloud of dust arising wherever the most action took place. Seeing these kids up close, B now noticed the stark difference in their conditions. Some wore only shorts, playing barefoot in the dirt, while others wore shoes and even some actual football jerseys. Talent levels varied as well; two or three older boys looked to B, around a year or two older than Moses, and they largely dominated the ball, weaving their way through the masses of other children. Every few minutes, a parent would appear on the hill near the tents, calling out a name and waving their hand, and a boy or girl would dart away, but there were also often more who would join. For what seemed like an hour, Moses and B ran and kicked and played, exuberant to be rid of their previous camp. Eventually, as enough children were called back to their parents, the energy of the game wound down, and the group began to wander toward water.

Small groups formed amongst the boys who knew each other, and B followed Moses into one group of four boys as they began to talk.

"My parents said that we may be leaving next week," one boy, taller and donning some sort of jersey, said.

"What?! My parents said we might be here for months—how are you leaving so soon?" another boy, presumably a friend of the first, responded.

"My dad has a college degree—he said that puts us at the top of the list. He even thinks we'll go to America," the first boy continued.

The eyes widened on the rest of the boys as they exclaimed in disbelief.

"What is America?" he asked, chiming into the conversation as he and Moses slightly trailed the group.

The four boys stopped their walk suddenly and turned their widened eyes to the Moises. Moses elbowed B, looking down begrudgingly at him for drawing such explicit attention to them both. The rest of the boys smiled, and they began to chime in, one after the other.

"America is like heaven," the boy with the jersey responded. "It goes heaven, America, and the rest of the world."

His other three friends smiled and chimed in their own perspectives on this mystical place.

"No one needs to work there!" one said.

"If you need money, you can just get it out of trash cans!"

"You don't need to own a car: you can just walk up to any one of them, and the keys are already there!"

"You can eat as much as you want, whenever you want!"

"Everyone gets a closet full of clothes!"

The statements kept shooting forth like bullets, and as B's eyes widened, his mind did as well, imagining this amazing new place. Finally, the boy with the jersey spoke again.

"But only the best of the best get to go to America. That's what this whole camp is for: deciding who gets to go. What does your father do?" he asked.

B's eyes quickly narrowed at the question, and his gaze turned down. He quickly glanced at Moses and saw the same response. The silence lasted for a few more seconds before being broken.

"Well, it doesn't sound like you'll be going to America anytime soon then!" the first boy responded, smiling and chuckling slightly. Without hesitation Moses jumped straight at him, grabbing him by his jersey. The other four boys quickly snatched the arms of Moses, preventing him from throwing a punch, but his grasp only strengthened. At once, Bikonzi felt a nervousness and a rush of adrenaline—he was ready to step in with and for his brother, even if they were to be a bit overmatched.

"You never speak of my father again," he yelled, eyes wide and neck bulging with anger, "or I'll make sure you can't ever get to America."

The boy in the jersey kept the smile on his face as Moses did, eventually squirming his way out of his grasp and pushing himself backward. Bikonzi wondered what it must have felt like for him to have protection and defenders on his side. He hadn't felt that, at least outside of his brothers and family, in months.

"You'd better be careful who you touch while you're here," he said once he was free, straightening out his crumpled clothes and strolling away surrounded by the other boys. Moses stood next to B, unmoving, staring as the boys walked away. Once they were at a reasonable distance, the brothers started back to their tent in silence. After a couple of minutes, B spoke up.

"America sounds amazing," he said, trying to divert the conversation from the conflict.

"If that kid will be there, then I don't want to go," Moses responded.

They finished their walk in silence, returning to the tent, retrieving their cups, and walking to a nearby spigot where they could pump water for themselves. As he sipped, B kept running the image of America through his head, imagining wide green soccer fields, cool, sunny weather, tables filled with fufu and rice and beef and fruits, and fresh, new clothes. As he did it, the clouds began to shout, drizzling rain forcing them to run, feet calloused and muddy, back to their tent for shelter.

CHAPTER 17:
GHOSTS

"When deed speaks, words are nothing."

-African Proverb

For B, the proceeding days were freeing. Their meals continued; he and Moses visited the soccer field nearly every afternoon, even in the rain and mud; he ran as often as he could. Yet as the sun set each day, darkness forced the Moises into their tent and B into his own heart and mind. For as much as he enjoyed the change he experienced here, he couldn't close his eyes in the stillness of the night without haunting images of the last year pressing in on him like an elephant into his chest. He knew all of this could disappear at any point.

Such wariness persisted across the whole family. While on the day of their arrival both Rose and John seemed relieved, passing time led to increased solemnity. B noticed it in their facial expressions: smiles were hard to come by, and they often spoke in hushed tones together in the evenings while everyone attempted to fall asleep. The ghost of Death kept Bikonzi awake, and he could overhear their words to one another.

"We're never getting out of here," John bemoaned one evening to Rose.

Rose remained silent, looking down as she fed Andre. John continued as if he hadn't been heard.

"No money…no education…no connection…no health…"

He held out a new finger with each new item on his list until Rose hushed him.

"Silence," she said as she glanced upward, eyes wide. She paused for a few seconds and spoke again.

"Did you think we'd make it here?" she asked.

Silence again.

"We wait. And we pray," she said, finishing the conversation.

B heard these words and it sent him into a spell of introspection. To this point, the notion of God being present, listening, or active in any sense in the middle of their suffering seemed naive to him and, at times, even infuriating to him. And yet this example of his mother, who had never wavered in her faith—and whose experience had clearly been more burdensome than his own—kept ringing in his heart like a blaring siren. He wondered if it had precisely been the faith that had enabled her to endure in the ways she did. He wondered how much of this endurance may have actually been God, in some unseen and quiet way, sustaining his mother through this. He wondered if the strength had actually come from God, contrary to the evidence that seemed to plead his absence. And, whether out of some inspiration from his mother's example or some woefully inadequate sense that God might just be there somewhere, Bikonzi began to pray himself. Eyes slammed shut, he pleaded in his head for all the things that arose: for health for Gelor and Andre, for more and better food, for freedom to America, for winning over the other boys in soccer, for his dad to return. He wasn't confident it would work, but he felt he needed it on this night. He fell asleep as his prayer trickled off like drops of water from a slowing spigot.

Over time, the boys who played on the soccer field started to disappear or were replaced by others. The boy who had bragged about his father was gone soon thereafter, and B's mind began to echo John's doubts. It wasn't helped by the continued malnourishment of the twins: even with more access to food, Gelor and Andre seemed to be getting worse each day—Rose's nourishment was hardly satisfactory, and it was showing up most in the twins.

A couple of weeks passed, and as B arrived back at the family's tent one day, he found a man and a woman crouched next to his mother. Yet these two were remarkably different than any people B had seen before. Their skin was pale and ghostly, and their hair was straight and long. When he walked in, they turned briefly to see him, and even their eyes were light. He couldn't help but continue staring.

After their short, shared glimpse, the man and woman turned back to Gelor and Andre, speaking to Rose in hushed tones. They wore white, with red crosses on their shirts. B approached the cot under which sat his food utensils, pretending to gather them together while he listened. After a few moments, the two stood and started to the tent flaps, smiling at Bikonzi as they walked. They stopped a few feet outside the tent and continued their conversation, but they spoke in a language B had not yet heard before. While he could not understand their words, he could tell from their tone that their conversation was urgent. After a few back-and-forth exchanges, they grew silent, and B could hear them stepping away.

"Bikonzi!" Rose quickly interjected. He was startled out of his eavesdropping. "Come, get your things. We are going for dinner."

B grabbed the utensils he had feigned searching for and joined Rose, John, and Moses in leading the family back to the food tent. As they walked, B noticed the same man and woman heading speedily in the other direction. One of them quickly turned back, making eye contact with them all, and then continued on.

That same night, B couldn't get to sleep quickly. He kept wondering about what might happen to Gelor and Andre. Who were those two? Why were they in such a rush? As he tossed the thoughts around in his mind, he heard a faint voice outside the tent, and his attention was diverted.

There was more than one voice, and they grew louder and nearer, though still muffled. Soon, damp footsteps joined with the voices—perhaps three people. B turned his body around, sitting up and resting upon his elbows. He was ready to jump at a moment's notice—he wouldn't be taken again. Squinting his eyes as they adjusted to the moonlit dark, he peered through the partially opened flaps in the tent as best he could. A few moments later, he noticed the frantic bouncing back and forth of a flashlight up against the white fabric. He braced himself even more, crouching now in a squat, ready to leap if needed. Then suddenly, a face poked through the flap, the same pale woman had made eye contact with him earlier that day. She still wore her red cross.

"Rose," she whispered urgently, repeating her name twice more.

B's mother sat up and rubbed the sleep from her eyes. The woman motioned to her to come. Rose immediately spoke to John.

"Gather your brothers and sisters. We're leaving."

Confused, B initially protested but was quickly quieted by John and Moses.

"There's no time," they said, "We're leaving."

Gathering themselves together, John grabbed Gelor while Rose held Andre. Moses and B held their siblings by the hand, and they each moved out into the darkness. They formed an imprecise line, weaving their way like a snake behind the leading flashlight at their front. B futility strained to see into the dark on this night, and he was forced to keep his eyes on Rose and follow.

Eventually, they broke through the mass of tents and out onto the road by which they had come before. A small white pickup truck was waiting there, and the woman with the flashlight urged them to jump into the bed as quickly as possible. The metal was cold against B's bare arms as he jumped in. John and Moses quickly worked to lift the littlest ones into the bed, jumping in and slamming the tailgate closed. The woman jumped into the passenger seat and spoke urgently to the driver, whom B could not make out. The truck churned and chugged to a start, and they were bumping their way along the route, back out underneath the banner they had entered under only a few days earlier. That same feeling of dread arrived back in his heart as the truck started up: piling into beds of trucks or the backs of planes had not exactly proven to lead to much prosperity to this point. Besides, he thought this place was a safe one—why the urgency if they were safe here? His questions bounced in his mind in the same way his body bounced in the truck as they continued.

They only drove for about 15 minutes and arrived at a small, one-story building adjacent to a long dirt strip. As they drew closer, B could hear the sound before he could make out the shape. The large engines of a plane were running, that high-pitched power ringing out in the darkness. As they approached, the shape of the plane came into form, looming over them. The truck drove immediately in the front of the aircraft and then ground to a halt in the mud as it drew closer.

The pale woman immediately jumped out of the passenger door, shouting in that same language he had not understood prior, waving her hands as she did. A front staircase descended down, and a man stepped confusedly out, shining a flashlight. She ran and spoke urgently to him, ascending the stairs and pointing back to the truck. The man shined his light toward the truck for a few moments, then re-entered the plane quickly. He returned with a clipboard, scanning over as the woman looked on. She shook her head as he did, but he insisted, shaking his head back. They shouted a few words back and forth to one another, and then, frustrated, the woman slapped the clipboard out of his hand. It clanged loudly down the stairs, heard even over the sound of the engines. The man stared at her in shock and silence, his eyes wide for a few moments. She spoke again, unflinching. He glanced back into the plane, then back at her, then once more at the truck. Finally, he motioned with his hands to her, and she swiftly returned to the Moises.

She spoke to Rose, transitioning to Lingala without a moment of hesitation. Under the churning noise of the plane and the truck, it was difficult to make out what they said, but Bikonzi could see his mother's expression: one of deep, tearful gratitude. After a few moments of their short conversation, which ended with an urgent embrace, the woman urged the rest of the family out of the truck and to the stairs.

They rushed again in their snake-line line, following the woman to the stairs. As they ascended the ramp, they entered the plane. This one was different than the last: peeking as best he could past the shoulder of John, he noticed amidst the dimmed lights cushioned chairs that lined each side, rows of three with an aisle in the middle. Dozens of other people filled that middle aisle, their arms and legs tightly held together and their eyes silently shining out amidst the darkness. No seats were left on the plane, so the Moises were told to sit in the aisle together. As they did, B could feel the eyes of the rest of the plane on them. He kept his gaze forward and down, strategically stepping between arms and legs and bodies lining the aisle. Eventually, they made it to the back of the plane, sitting together in a straight line. As he turned and took his place, B looked up to the front of the plane and caught a glimpse of that same woman, who had turned back over her shoulder one last time, smiling slightly before descending the stairs and back to the white truck. Then the door closed behind her, and the man to whom she had spoken disappeared behind a door at the front of the plane. It began to move, and within minutes, they were speeding upwards again. B had to grasp the seats adjacent to him to keep from rolling back down as they ascended. After about 30 minutes, they had finally leveled out, and B whispered to Rose.

"Mom—where are we going?"

She paused only slightly, as if she needed to catch her breath.

"America," she said.

CHAPTER 18:

HOME

"A bird that flies off the earth and lands on an anthill is still on the ground."

-African Proverb

The night passed slowly. After only a few minutes, the Moises had spread out, scattering themselves across the aisle and running up and down the plane. B lay in the fetal position as best he could for as long as he could, but the occasional turbulence or kick from someone sitting on the plane regularly woke him. These moments interrupted his dreams. In between sleep, he recalled all of the visions of America that the boys had spoken of at the soccer field. Images of cars, of full tables of food, of sunshine and clean clothes filled his mind on that dark evening. They were the best dreams he had had in years. And yet he remained doubtful. After these last few months, he found himself hesitant to trust any story that wasn't in some way dictated by Death. And besides, could it really be that his family had been chosen, amongst all the others, for this journey? How could this have happened to them? They weren't exactly the most qualified, at least based on the criteria that John had seemed to indicate. Hours passed as he wrestled back and forth, with sleep hard to come by, dreams fast and free, and doubts arriving in his heart and mind at the same pace. Eventually the sun began to shine through the small and open windows on the aircraft. Heat emanated through the walls and floor as it did—B could feel it on his skin. The heat intensified as the sun rose, and soon, beads of sweat appeared on his forehead. As the heat turned up, the plane began its descent, bouncing its way through the air and violently screeching to a halt upon the ground. A muffled voice spoke in English from somewhere around them, loud enough for the whole plane to hear.

As soon as the voice had finished, the rest of the plane broke into a frenzy. Everyone frantically spoke and pushed; some attempted to step over the Moises as they jockeyed for the front door. B stood up and pushed back against these others where he could, though he was easily cast aside by the men and boys older and stronger than him who shoved forward. Slowly, this mass of bodies funneled their way to the front door and descended the stairs. The Moises became separated amidst the shoving, and John waited adjacent to the bottom of the stairs to ensure no one was missed. He pulled them all into a huddle on the asphalt tarmac, which was already burning their feet, reflecting the aggressive sun above them and emanating up through the bottoms of their sandals. Once they gathered together, they huddled to the closest building, following the crowd. B stepped as lightly as possible, trying to avoid as much contact with the scalding ground as he could.

Along their way, they noticed a dozen or so well-dressed individuals, many wearing sunglasses, lined up on either side of the crowd. They called out names, and some of them held signs or placards up as well. The crowd began to dwindle in size as they all walked along, with couples and families veering off, presumably in response to the name-callers. Then, in the flurry of words and names, B heard one that was particularly familiar.

"Moises!"

At first, he wasn't sure if he heard it right. It didn't seem that Rose or John had heard it either, so he ignored it and kept walking. But then it rang out again.

"Moises!"

This second call was unmistakable to the family. They started swiveling glances back and forth, trying to pinpoint the source when it was called a third time.

"Moises!"

B heard clearly where the name was coming from this time. He turned to his right and saw an older man dressed nicely in a green collared shirt wrapped in a gray jacket and jeans. His hair was peppered with gray and trimmed short, and his eyes matched his deep brown skin. B called out when he spotted the man.

"Mom! Here!" he said, pointing as he did.

Rose turned, saw where B pointed and started toward the man, the family following. They gathered around him, still confused yet comforted by the hearing of their own name. After the family drew near, the man started speaking:

"Are you the Moise family?" he asked, speaking in Swahili. B was relieved to be talking with someone he could understand.

"Yes," Rose replied, looking down and motioning to all her children, "Yes, we are."

"Excellent," he replied, "My name is Augustine. Welcome to America. Let's get you all out of the sun, yes?"

He kindly smiled after this last comment, motioning for the family to follow him. They continued to walking, and upon entering the doors, they were greeted by a long, winding line that worked its way to a series of glass booths. Hundreds of people stood in the line: B recognized some of them from the previous plane ride, but many others were quite different. More pale people caught his eye, and he wondered where these sorts of people had come from. The line moved slowly, with each person taking one or two steps forward every couple of minutes. B also noticed a uniformed man residing in each booth, and while their uniforms shined a bright blue and looked cleaner, their facial expressions reminded him of the guards from the camp. This kept his gaze fixed upon those booths: he nervously darted his eyes to each of these men in tandem.

"We'll need to wait in this line for a bit—should only take around an hour to get through," Augustine spoke to Rose.

The proceeding minutes crawled by, step by step. At times, folks arrived at the glass booths in exhaustion and were quickly moved past them; other times, there were loud and abrasive arguments at the booth. One man needed to be pulled away by two other uniformed men because of his yelling and pointing. All the while, the line kept moving.

Eventually, they made their way to the front, and Augustine turned briefly to Rose.

"I'll speak for you all—don't worry about responding directly."

Augustine then stepped forward, and B was drawn to the remarkable patience he displayed as he approached the glass booth. His voice quickly changed to speak a different language to the man in the booth, and the warmth of his eyes and his smile calmly moved their conversation back and forth. He motioned a couple of times back to the Moises, and the guard stood from his seat and glanced them over with skeptical eyes. At one point Augustine took a series of documents from his jacket pocket, sliding them to the man behind the glass. He looked them over, silently scanning the papers while Augustine waited diligently. Then, after a couple of minutes, the guard snapped free from his scanning, nodded, and motioned with his hand forward. Without delay, Augustine turned back to Rose and, with his arms motioning the family together, stated shortly:

"Come—this way."

They followed him through a shiny metal gate with rotating bars that each of the family members had to push their way through. This led to more walking, and B was amazed by the building's new, shiny, and expansive nature. They walked through broad and high hallways, with hundreds of people scurrying back and forth on their business, rolling or carrying bags as they went. They stepped on the thin and coarse carpet, which was nevertheless a welcome gift after the harsh, hot tarmac from which they had arrived. Every once in a while, a person would turn and notice the Moises, staring for a few moments in a break from their own routine, only to return again to the world of their own busyness. There were huge glass windows that appeared on either side of them at points, visual portals to the runways with planes taking off and landing. Adjacent to these windows going each direction were sections of railings, held up by glass and metal, lining the sides of the ground that, to B's surprise, moved. When they arrived at one of these, Bikonzi was quite confused: some people stood a few dozen feet in front of them who were simply standing, yet moving forward. Augustine invited the Moises onto the moving ground happily, and they each cautiously stepped forward, holding tightly onto the railing as they did.

They rode this down the extended corridors, and after they stepped off the man weaved the Moises in and through some remaining crowds, deftly ensuring they remained together while also keeping them moving forward. Finally, they turned a corner to an alcove, which saw three sets of metal doors and small metal buttons adjacent to them. B had never seen such things. Augustine pressed one of the buttons, and after a few moments, the two metal doors opened with a ding and a low rumbling. Augustine stepped through the doors, and Moises followed cautiously again, stepping through the doorway into a small, boxed room with more buttons and symbols on the side wall. Augustine pressed another button, and the room jolted, beginning to move. Bikonzi felt a weird lightness in his belly as it did, and after a few moments, the room jolted to a stop, and the doors opened once again.

This time, they stepped out into a dimly lit, dark concrete space with lines of cars that went as far as Bikonzi could see. Augustine moved them quickly down one of the rows of cars, eventually arriving at a large white van. He slid the side door open, revealing three rows of cushioned seats proceeding toward the back of the van. The Moises piled in, Augustine took a front seat behind the wheel, and they were off. Winding their way out of the dark garage, they opened up into a bright and busy area. B looked out the window of the van to see dozens of cars speeding around them, moving seemingly without reason across yellow and white painted lines on the ground. Augustine seemed to have an idea of where he wanted to go, but to B, it only looked like chaos. He turned forward and noticed a mirror, which reflected his mother's eyes back to him. They, too, were scanning the streets around them, at once excited and decidedly nervous.

Their drive took only about ten minutes, with Augustine expertly winding through the chaotic freeways and streets around them. Eventually, they arrived at a neighborhood where Augustine slowed his speed; his head turned to the right as he neared their destination. Still peering out the window, B saw on both sides of the street buildings that stood three and sometimes four levels tall, all the same color and woven together, tucked behind rusty metal gates. Augustine pulled up to one of these rusted gates to the right, pulling the van up close; suddenly, the gate started moving, opening enough space for Augustine to pull the van through. They drove slowly, bumping their way over humps in the road, with cars lining the van to their right and an expansive four-story collection of buildings to their left. They wound their way around these buildings until Augustine eventually pulled into a parking spot. He instructed them out of the van and to follow him. They walked toward the nearest building, which had a staircase connected to the side. The family climbed up to the third floor of the building, following Augustine down a covered outdoor corridor, passing a multitude of doors along the way. Eventually, Augustine stopped outside of one of the doors, pulled keys from his pocket, jiggled them within the golden door handle, and squeaked the door open. He extended his arm forward, flipped on a light switch inside, smiled at Rose and John, and spoke only one word:

"Welcome."

B moved forward with each of his family members to the doorway, cautiously approaching it in the same manner they approached the elements in the airport. They stepped first onto beige shag carpeting, with burnt yellow walls and a textured ceiling that, to Bikonzi, looked like cottage cheese. To the right was a couch and light brown wooden table, and to the left a television standing alone on a stand. Peering just past this room, they saw a kitchen with light brown cabinets and a small table underneath a glass lamp hanging from the ceiling. As they all moved through the carpeted room to the kitchen, they noticed on their left a hallway corridor.

They followed it together: it led to one doorway and opening on the left, one on the right, and one at the end of the hallway. Each room had multiple beds, a dresser, and a closet, and one of the rooms even had toys: a soccer ball caught B's eye, as did a collection of small trucks and cars.

Rose was silent as they moved through the place, bouncing a lightly crying Andre as she did. Each of the children followed her lead, silently falling in line, and they all eventually returned to the first carpeted room, where Augustine stood, smiling slightly with his hands resting in his pockets.

"There's food in the refrigerator," he said, motioning toward the kitchen.

At the sound of the word food, B's stomach growled loudly, and he looked up with Moses to Rose. She glanced down at them, smiled, and nodded, and the boys, without hesitation, sprinted to the refrigerator, elbowing and shoving one another as they did.

Augustine had understated things. Upon opening the door, B was overcome by the colorful canvas that sat in front of him. Fruits and vegetables, milk and juice, bread, meat, and cheese filled the space. An instinctual and unutterable joy filled his chest as his eyes widened at the sight. He and Moses grabbed frantically for what they could, filling their arms as full as possible and scattering it all upon the table. They sat at the elevated chairs there for a few minutes to eat, and B heard Augustine and Rose laugh lightly as they spoke together. Finally, upon stuffing themselves, B turned his full attention back to the rest of his family. Augustine had left, seemingly without noise, and Rose and John were holding and bouncing back and forth with Gelor and Andre in their arms. Both were smiling and cooing, happiness emanating from their playful postures. Seth and Team had managed to work their way to the bedroom and bring some of the toys they had noticed down the hallway; trucks and balls rattled and bounced around the carpet, and a chorus of laughs rang through the small place.

Eventually, following this initial raid of Moses and Bikonzi, John approached the kitchen. He opened two of the cabinets to find plates and glasses there, and one of the drawers revealed knives and forks as well. John proceeded to make two sandwiches, cut some fruit and vegetables, and carried them over to Rose, setting them on the table and releasing his weight onto the couch as he did. Rose began to feed Gelor and Andre while John invited Seth and Team to him to consume a bit of what he had cut.

B went over to the carpet and collapsed his body down onto the shag cushioning. He closed his eyes and felt it enveloping his back and arms. He moved his hands slowly through its texture. Chills ran down his arms and legs, followed quickly by a deep warming that filled his whole body. He took a deep breath, his chest expanding as far as it could go, and then he simply let it sigh out. As he did, the last few months rushed back into his heart and mind, a strange fusion of gratitude and grief.

In one sense, the food, the place, the refrigerator, the softness of the ground upon which he now laid—all of them came together to make Bikonzi feel, in many ways, at peace. But the longer he laid here, the more questions and insecurity sparked a sense of grief in him. This wasn't, after all, home; even on the shag carpeting, he missed those black-and-white tiled floors of home. He missed the green trees, the mystery and wonder of the dense forests of his homeland, which were replaced by this dry and arid place in which they now had been forced to settle. He missed his father, his school, his church, his life. How was he to proceed from here? Everyone he had seen so far spoke a different language; everyone he had seen looked and dressed utterly differently; everyone was not him or his people.

And so he felt, somewhere in his inner and unutterable reaches, in a world between homes—a home that had been ripped away from him and a new one offered that could never truly be replaced. He felt a full belly and a wandering heart.

As these reflections boiled up in him, he opened his eyes and raised his head to his mother; his body splayed out upon the carpet. He uttered a question that was both inadequate and necessary.

"Mother," he started, "Is this home?"

She was feeding Andre when he asked, and her gaze was fixed happily upon his small face. She waited a few moments before responding. Then, without moving her eyes and with a warmth in her voice just like the carpet that B laid upon, Rose replied:

"No. Not truly, my son. It won't feel like home, and that's okay. But together we can try and make it so. Together, we can try and make it so."

Bikonzi paused upon his mother's face for a moment and allowed her words to settle in to his mind and heart. He lowered his head back to his carpeted pillow and stared toward the textured ceiling, the ridges winding wildly across his line of sight. He'd try and make it so.

CHAPTER 19: NZAMBE

"To be hated by a human being is not to be hated by God."

-African Proverb

After a few months, Bikonzi's best intentions had hardly worked to make this new place home in any real sense. While he slowly strengthened with marginally better nutrition, their newness to the country meant they still had little to spend on groceries, and so he carried the toll of his time in the camp in his body: his arms were thin, his chest a board, and his face long and narrowed. While he had started school nearby with his siblings, the place felt more foreign to him at times than even the camp: few people shared his family's dark, black skin; others' clothes were regularly nicer and newer than the thrifted cotton t-shirts and athletic shorts they had been forced to buy with the little money they had; their language was a strange and foreign one. It struck Bikonzi that even with the language barrier, his new peers at school still managed to communicate via sneers and unknown jokes, nonverbal distancing during classes and breaks, and behavior that felt as distancing and belittling as that of the guards from the camp. He quickly learned that physical violence isn't the only type.

This new place—Phoenix, Arizona, which he had learned to say in English—even had a climate that felt alienating. The air was dry: it had not rained since they had arrived, and the few clouds that graced the expansive blue sky were often whisps of white, mere footnotes to the dense, filled rainclouds of his home. He saw bland beige everywhere he looked, with gray rocks and thorny trees replacing the lush and thick greens he knew. As the summer arrived, it became nearly unbearable to venture outdoors at all, an unrelenting sun almost piercing their skin with heat.

Though she carried herself with enduring strength, Bikonzi could tell Rose felt the weight of the transition as well. She would take the bus numerous times weekly to a nearby center where she could learn English and, out of necessity, would often bring along at least two of her children. Bikonzi would join occasionally for Saturday or Sunday trips to the center. Such distractions could only prolong her learning, particularly in the case of the twins: still recovering from malnourishment, they often required intensive attention, and Rose was even forced to take numerous trips to the hospital for them in those first few months.

Then, one day, in the middle of a week of blazing heat, thick and imposing gray clouds moved in upon the city. After making his way to school in the morning, Bikonzi looked out his window during his first hour, drawn by the unseen and booming thunderclaps of the sky. Suddenly, as he peered out the school window, rain dumped down in buckets as if all poured out at once. Feigning attention in his class—he couldn't understand much of what the teacher was saying anyway—he watched as the ground, within minutes, was flooded by the downpour. This was different than the rain at home, where the water came in slower, lighter, more perpetual waves, but he nonetheless found his heart strangely softened by the storm. M*aybe something could grow in this desolate desert after all,* he thought to himself. At least, for a moment, things felt a bit like home.

The storm continued off and on for the rest of the day. That afternoon, after his own bus ride home, his mother returned from her latest English lesson, twins in hand. Her hair and clothes dripped as she stepped inside, but she seemed lighter and hopeful, with more bounce in her step than usual. She had a large smile cast across her face as she started to speak.

"Children," she called out to Bikonzi and his siblings, who were all scattered around the apartment. "I have good news."

They huddled together around her, ears attentive as she set down the twins and they crawled their way to Amiee and John.

"I met a woman today at my class—she is a volunteer French teacher who was speaking just next door to my English class."

This, on its own, was a remarkable revelation: while his own French was nearly entirely absent, Bikonzi knew his mother was fluent. This may have been one of the first women with whom she could have held a full conversation since they had arrived.

"I told her our story: where we are from, where we are living, where you all go to school. Then, as we were leaving, she noticed that I was walking to the uncovered bus stop in the rain to wait, and she offered me a ride home. We kept talking, and she invited us to spend time with her and her husband this weekend at the park!"

Initially off-put by the prospect of meeting more new strangers, Rose's final comment piqued Bikonzi's interest:

"They're going to grill some hamburgers for us," she said.

The weekend came slowly as the week at school finished, but in the late morning Saturday, the Moises were greeted by the sound of a gentle knock at their door.

"Get your things together!" she commanded to the room, holding Gelor as she moved to answer. While Moses grabbed their well-worn soccer ball, and Amiee and John gathered the younger siblings together with a dozen or so Sprite cans from the refrigerator, Bikonzi traversed cautiously behind his mother to the door. He wanted to see this strange woman that Rose had spoken about.

After arriving at the door, Rose opened it gently, and was greeted by a kind voice, speaking in French words that even Bikonzi knew.

"Hello, Rose!" the woman spoke warmly as she embraced his mother in a hug. She spoke a few other words to her that Bikonzi couldn't understand, and then turned her gaze toward him. In the midst of trailing his mother, Bikonzi didn't realize how close he had actually gotten to the door: he stood only a couple of feet behind his mother's left leg, staring and evaluating the woman. She was short in comparison to Rose, with tight curly hair and skin only slightly lighter; her voice carried a soft and calming tone, and as she turned to Bikonzi, a welcoming greeting emanated from her red lips.

"Hello—are you Bikonzi?" she asked him.

He didn't answer verbally, opting to nod his head in affirmation.

"I'm glad to meet you…" she said, and though she continued talking, Bikonzi could not understand the rest of her words, and so he nodded again in response. Even in a language he could not understand, her speech felt like a breath of fresh air in his chest. It was opening, expanding, refreshing. He felt seen then rather than cast aside like he had at school.

"Let's go!" Rose called out again as her children trailed behind her. They walked their way down their outdoor apartment stairs to an already running navy blue van, which sat in front of a silver SUV. The woman stepped into the driver's seat of the latter while another man sat in the driver's seat of the former. Car seats had already been loaded into the SUV, so Rose took the passenger seat there and inserted the smallest siblings into the car seats with the woman's help. Meanwhile, Amiee, John, Moses, and Bikonzi all joined the minivan, greeted by the words of the man as they did.

"You can call me Brother Tony," he said as the older siblings stepped into the vehicle. After these few months, B had at least learned how to perceive name introductions, and so he understood Tony's statement. "And that woman," Brother Tony pointed back to the SUV behind them, prompting each of them to turn back, "That's my wife—you can call her Mama Dee."

Brother Tony was much larger than his wife. Though seated, Bikonzi was struck by his broad, thick, muscular build and deep, powerful voice: he carried a calm and caring strength that prompted a feeling of safety, even in their first exchange.

They arrived at the park after only a few minutes. Anxious to get out of the silent and awkward car ride, Bikonzi and Moses immediately leaped from the car and strode to a nearby wooden and worn picnic table, sitting in the shade of a pine tree—beads of perspiration already ran down their foreheads as they dropped their soccer ball and kicked back and forth in the desert sun. Over the next few minutes, between kicks and passes together, Bikonzi noticed Brother Tony's trips back and forth to the minivan. Numerous large bags, a blue and white cooler, chips, and drinks all came with him from the back of the minivan, and after a few minutes, he started grilling. The scent of hot dogs and burgers wafted to the boys, who—after only a few minutes—were already well-drenched in sweat, and they slowly worked their way back to the shaded table.

As they did, Brother Tony noticed them and–stepping away from the grill–lifted up the top of the cooler, reaching in and grabbing two bottles of yellow Gatorade. He handed them to Moses and Bikonzi, wordlessly smiling as he did. Upon taking them and responding "Thank you"–one of the phrases they had learned in English to this point–they cracked open the orange lids and, without hesitation, gulped them down. Bikonzi immediately noticed how cold they were: there were small, slow beads of melted ice dripping down the sides of the bottle, cooling his hand, and the sweet and sugary liquid ran down his throat with refreshing speed.

After quickly chugging half a bottle each, he and Moses collapsed down onto benches of the picnic table, now noticing a smattering of chips and plates that had already been dug into by his siblings, mother, and Mama Dee, the latter two now immersed in conversation with one another. He passed on the plate, opting instead to shove his hand in the bag and grab as large a handful of chips as he could. His hand emerged from the bag and went straight to his mouth, salty shrapnel dropping along the way, and the flavor-packed crunch served as a fitting complement to his cool, sugary drink. Sipping a bit more, Bikonzi now turned outward toward the park, taking in the scene.

Amiee was sitting just to his right, her legs crisscrossed beneath her pregnant belly upon a blanket, and she giggled as she played with a crawling Andre. John stood quietly just next to her, holding a plate and slowly snacking on chips as he looked off into the distance around the rest of the park. Seth and Team danced around in the shade, heartedly laughing and playing tag with one another.

It was there, in the shaded pine of that Saturday morning, that Bikonzi felt his heart strangely warmed. The honoring gaze of Mama Dee and Brother Tony, in a place where he had felt utterly invisible, had made him and his family visible, known, and real once again, filling his chest with a sense of self. And he wondered again about God. In his lemon-lime sips and salty bites, in his smiling, sweat-laden play, in the words and actions of this strange and lovely couple that communicated before they were understood, Bikonzi knew this was God. And in the fluttering and unutterable half-thoughts bouncing between his heart and mind, he knew something in him was healing. Certainly not done, and certainly not perfect, and yet—healing. He smiled as he lifted his drink to his lips again, and he recalled again those words his mother so often had spoken in prayer, in Lingala, the same words she had spoken on that night they were taken: thanks to God, to Nzambe. Gratitude. He wondered if it was there, in some still and secret way, that this healing began in him.

And so, almost without conscious thought, he softly uttered those words that arose only from some deep inner spring he had only just started to unearth along the way these last few months.

Webale, Nzambe. Webale.

AFTERWORD

"A friend is someone you share the path with."

-African Proverb

I first met Bikonzi as an undergraduate freshman at the university we attended together. We lived on the same dorm room floor, and so would exchange casual nods and greetings in passing one another during our first semester there. These friendly and knowing glances evolved into deeper friendship after we encountered each other in a far less casual location later on: the basketball courts at the campus rec center. I've grown up competitive - I can't remember a time in my life where I wasn't compelled to push myself to the final inch of my capacity in order to win anything, from board games to baseball and beyond, but in these moments on the basketball court, I realized I may have found someone whose competitive instincts even superseded mine. Bikonzi was an absolute hooper.

And so pickup basketball became a regular rhythm for us. I quickly learned that being on Bikonzi's team was a far more enjoyable endeavor than competing against him: first, because his size (6'4" and nothing but lean muscle) and skills made him physically imposing to guard if you were, like me, a 6'1" skinny white kid; but second, and more importantly, if you played with Bikonzi, he'd regularly set you up with open shots. I gladly took on the role of outside shooter and hard-working defender to Bikonzi's playmaking and scoring, and over those few weeks, we continued to hone our competitive kindred spirit alongside a collection of other teammates and friends we remain close with today.

It wasn't until Spring Break during that same freshman year that I first heard the fuller version of his story. We traveled from Phoenix to California with two other close friends, where we stayed at the vacated home of one of their parents. There is perhaps no better formula for developing a friend–and, I would imagine, an enemy–than six hours in a car, followed by a week of constant competition traversing from beach to pickup basketball game to beach again. Despite our many arguments and competitive battles—I'd like to note my game-winning three over Bikonzi in a pickup game on this trip, just to ensure it is on the record—it was in this close proximity that we became far more friends than enemies, sharing our life stories in between all the action: our struggles, our joys, our passions, our relationship histories, our faith and dreams and questions and doubts and the rest.

In our years throughout the rest of college, this friendship led to a shattering of my own relatively sheltered, suburban experience in life. I learned the ins and outs of my friend's refugee and resettlement experience; I learned the manifold struggles that he and his family had to endure and overcome; I learned, slowly through an abundance of interactions and questions and stumbling on my part, about Congolese culture and heritage; and, more than this, I learned of a faith that sustained him and from which he drew strength in every area of his life.

As our college years together neared an end, Bikonzi approached me with a proposition. Knowing I was an English major with aspirations to write and publish at some point in my still completely unknown future and having read a few of my essays and other short fiction pieces, he asked if I would like to partner with him in writing and publishing his story. My immediate response was simultaneous honor and terror: honor because of the trust he had in me to help be a major creative voice in telling his story, and terror because I was certainly not qualified to tell it well. I expressed both these sentiments to him, only to have his trust in me reinforced: he wanted *me* to write the book and had no aim to try and push it off to another writer.

Before I simply embraced the task, we took some time over the preceding year or so to discuss some of the reasons behind his desire to write the book. Why was it important for him to tell his story in this way, from his perspective? And why now, as his story was still being written? Where do we start, and where do we end, it our telling? What did he hope for as an end result? Who was his audience? These sorts of questions helped he and I hone the vision more clearly, and eventually, I accepted his offer to write.

Extensive interviews and research proceeded. I had the privilege interviewing B's mother and older siblings, all of whom provided powerful stories and testimonies of their own that broadened my understanding of the family's experience. I dove into the history of Congo which preceded the First and Second Congo Wars, all parts of history that much of our Western American education is entirely silent about. As a brief note, I am greatly indebted to Gérard Prunier's *Africa's World War: Congo, The Rwandan Genocide, and the Making of a Continental Catastophe,* Jason K. Stearn's *Dancing In The Glory of Monsters: The Collapse of the Congo and the Great War of Africa*, and the works of Congolese historians like Jacques Depelchin Isidore Ndaywel è Nziem. This book doesn't get written without these tremendous historians doing terrific work on a far too overlooked aspect of world history.

Much of this work was slow going, as it happened alongside full-time work for Bikonzi and me, the starting of each of our families, and graduate school for myself. Not only this, the nature of the story proved challenging to manifest, as it centralized a young boy who, while aware of many of the dynamics that had created his family's situation, was not clued into everything in the moment. One of the primary writing challenges for me was maintaining Bikonzi's point of view while giving enough context clues and notes that the modern Western reader would still be able to grasp some of the dynamics with clarity. The result, at certain points, involved more "showing" than "telling," inviting the reader to wonder, alongside Bikonzi, why things were happening in the way they were. While this helps the story's pacing throughout, I did feel it could be helpful to provide some notes here, in an epilogue, on the more explicitly biographical details to help fill any gaps readers might have.

We decided to start the book the night the Moise family was taken from their home and end the book as they attempted to resettle in a place not their home, effectively bookending their story as a way of relating the refugee experience of home–and lack thereof–to the reader. Tribally Tutsi, the Moises were a staple of Christian charity and neighbor love in their community but found themselves eventually caught in the crossfires of tribal conflicts that had been largely initiated and amplified by European settlers in the decades prior. While these conflicts were most prominent in the tragic Rwandan genocide of the 1990s, they also leaked into surrounding nations, including the Moise's home of the Democratic Republic of Congo (DRC). On August 2nd, 1998, the government of the DRC ordered the systemic persecution of the Tutsi people, and this prompted regular police visits to the Moise home. Rose and her husband initially believed that the primary goal of these officers was simply to take the family's patriarch and money away, and so they worked to hide his presence in the home, lying when officers visited; however, after a T.V. broadcast proclaimed that the president had ordered the killing of Tutsi families and the looting of their possessions, the Moises had to go into deeper hiding. They cloaked their home in darkness, paying friends and family to make any purchases they needed to give the impression that their home was abandoned.

While this worked for a short time, eventually, they were exposed. Traya, whose own family had been subject to this same persecution and had already been taken captive, chose to reveal the Moise location to the officers in their community. On September 23, 1998, officers broke into their home and took the family away. While his father fled, he was eventually caught and killed, unable to navigate the rest of the journey with his family. After a few short nights in their local jail, they were transported to the concentration camp, where much of our story here takes place. The conditions were utterly miserable and dehumanizing, and the selection of stories we include here are intended to be representative of this state from the perspective of Bikonzi at the time. While in the camp, two major events utterly altered the fate of the family.

The first was the birth of the twins. Rose labored in the middle of the night without any medical attention and amidst the horribly unsanitary conditions of the warehouse in which they were being kept. After giving birth, she tied the umbilical cords using the thread that bound her hair and cut them with a piece of wood she had found nearby. Knowing that the children's survival was unlikely in such conditions, and in an attempt to embody the forgiveness central to her own faith, she decided to name the children after the two commanding officers of the camp. Given the cultural significance of namesakes, her risk paid off for her family: the wives of the commanding officers showed compassion on them, bringing food and other materials, and eventually, they were transferred from the camp, as the commanders did not want to be directly responsible for the killing of their namesakes.

The second factor in their survival was Amiee's story. During their time at the camp, one of the guards took a liking to Amiee, and in an exchange that prevented the guards from taking John away, Amiee was given away to be a partner for this man. Eventually, she became pregnant, and so now, an additional guard at the camp had a vested interest in keeping the Moise family free from violence. This guard—in conversation with Joseph Kabila, the son of then DRC president Laurent-Désiré Kabila—worked to have them transferred away from the camp, and we depict this scene from Bikonzi's perspective in the final conversation as Amiee is returned to the family and her pregnancy is revealed.

These two instances ultimately led the family to, eventually, be transferred to the Cameroonian Red Cross center, where the compassionate actions of Sasha and Shaeka—who play a crucial role in this book while remaining unnamed–ultimately led the Moise family to gain refugee status in July 2000, moving them to Phoenix, where they reside today. While this move was certainly a reprieve, it nonetheless placed them unpreparedly in an entirely foreign land, which proved challenging in its own right. While we chose to stop the book where we did, Bikonzi and I have spoken extensively about writing a sequel that explores the challenges of the resettlement process for the family here in the U.S. It was not an immediate "happily ever after," and Bikonzi has expressed that one of the greatest needs for Western ears is to hear the trials of resettlement so that they might be motivated to step in and help embody hospitality and compassion when able, as Brother Tony and Mama Dee did so effectively for years with the Moises. Rose now works to raise public awareness and funds for those displaced around the world; her story has been featured in the documentary *Pushing The Elephant*, and she has been interviewed about her story by outlets like NPR and the UN Refugee Agency, amongst others. Bikonzi's faith continues to play a central role in his life, as he works today with an organization called MissionOne to help support the local church in locales around the world to bring flourishing and life to all peoples.

All along the journey of writing this book, in my own doubts and preconceptions about my shortcomings in progress, Bikonzi's support and friendship were the regular force that kept the text moving along, as he routinely articulated his trust in me to tell the story well. Upon completing graduate school, I got to work in earnest on the foundations of the project you read here, and it was in this season, he and I landed on our ultimate hopes and goals for this book. The literary choices we made throughout—from genre to language to point of view—were all ultimately rooted in these goals, and we felt it would be helpful to list them more explicitly here:

First, to provide a clear-minded, evocative examination of a part of world history often overlooked by Western, American audiences: the intimacy of the point of view in this book was borne out of the intentional desire we had to avoid abstracting the experiences of many people during the First and Second Congo War. A biography, or even a historical examination, certainly has its place, but given Bikonzi's unique perspective, we felt that a nonfiction narrative format would speak to the heart and keep us from turning this conflict into strictly data and statistics.

Second, to promote the importance of action in the West when it comes to refugee resettlement: in recent years, particularly in America, negative, dismissive, and even outright xenophobic language has become increasingly commonplace in response to the conflicts happening around the world and the countless people fleeing their homes in the midst of such conflicts. The result is often, at best, naivete and, at worst, indifference when it comes to understanding refugee stories and helping displaced neighbors. There are an abundance of organizations and resources available on this front that we will provide at the end of this note: these all help to provide tangible and actionable clarity on the best ways to show up for our refugee neighbors. Our hope is that this book serves as a catalyst to get more involved in the lives of the displaced all around you in your local community.

Third, to tell Bikonzi's story in a way that can be passed down to his future generations: from a more personal angle, our hope with this book is that Bikonzi's unique story and perspective can be preserved so that his children, grandchildren, and great-grandchildren can trace their family's connections in a way that at once roots them in their cultural history and also energizes them in their present.

Fourth, to encourage readers to consider the role of faith in suffering: as it likely evident throughout the text for those who read it, the dance between faith and doubt plays a central role in Bikonzi and his family's story. In many ways, these fundamental (and universally human) principles are the building blocks for any healthy navigation of our suffering, and our hope is that—independent of where you land in your own spiritual journey—you would find these texts to be a helpful encouragement to explore more deeply the way that faith might drive you to deal with your pain and suffering in healing and life-giving ways.

We are also fully aware that any work of art, once it is completed, will take on a life of its own in the mind and heart of the audience. We thus fully expect that you, the reader, will walk away with a flurry of other observations and takeaways—in fact, we hope that will happen and that this book will open up streams of reflection and thought completely unforeseen to us upon our writing of it. More than anything, we want to thank you for purchasing and reading this book and for your continued care and support for all neighbors who are marginalized and vulnerable nearby and around the world. May we continue to work together for the flourishing and peace of our world, remembering always that we belong to one another.

Grace,
Clint Leavitt

CALL TO ACTION

Refugee Relief and Resettlement Organization Recommendations

UN Refugee Agency

Catholic Relief Services

United States Refugee Resettlement Partners Through UN

World Relief

Lifting Hands International

Relief International

Miles4Migrants

ABOUT THE AUTHOR

Rev. Clint Leavitt is a pastor, professor, author, and poet who believes stories are the key to our way back home–to the Way, the Truth, and the Life. With an undergraduate degree in English Literature and a Master's in Theology and Culture from Fuller Theological Seminary, Clint now serves as the pastor of Midtown Presbyterian Church and as a professor and curriculum developer for undergraduate students at Grand Canyon University, helping to write and teach classes like Christianity and Culture, Christian Worldview and Media, World Religions, Pentateuch, and more. He loves literature and film, writing reviews on his own personal site and for Loud and Clear Reviews, and all things sports, watching and playing whenever he has space. He lives in Phoenix, AZ, with his wife Emily, daughter Zoe, and Goldendoodle companion, Wally.

www.ingramcontent.com/pod-product-compliance
Lightning Source LLC
LaVergne TN
LVHW090613060525
810463LV00004B/22
9781636986852